"Every conversation in this book I had a. I didn't have this book to ground and launch those discussions. If you are a college student or work with them, then this is the book to get together to discuss and wrestle with what it looks like to follow Jesus in the face of a dominant culture that calls you to look elsewhere for identity, significance, and satisfaction."

Jonathan P. Walton, area director, InterVarsity/USA, author of *Twelve Lies That Hold America Captive: And the Truth That Sets Us Free*

"Every church that sends its kids off to college and every parent who wants their child to navigate the higher education experience as a disciple of Jesus should give them a compass and this book. Both will help the matriculating student stay on course—in the case of this book, not with canned advice, as is so often the case, but with deep wisdom, honest reflections, and practical advice about the most significant questions that often haunt Christian students, whether they attend secular or religious institutions. In any case, every Christian college should make this book required reading during its students' first semester."

Dennis Okholm, Azusa Pacific University, author of *Learning Theology Through the Church's Worship*

"To have within a single volume twelve different experts, whose own lives and callings have been indelibly shaped by their Christian faith, winsomely and honestly translate their expertise into practical wisdom for following Jesus in the contours, struggles, and questions of everyday life—the result is a pearl of great price, one book worth innumerable other books. I can think of so many Christians navigating the very present questions and challenges that arise over the course of life, from confronting suffering to figuring out if church really matters to engaging in activism, who I would want to benefit from the wisdom of this book. The importance of the topics that are engaged, the ways those topics are shaped by the real-life experiences of those writing, and the clear compassion that permeates the engagement combine together to make this a must-read book for college students, twenty- and thirtysomethings, and those well beyond."

Kristen Deede Johnson, dean and professor of theology and Christian formation at Western Theological Seminary

"Despite stereotypes, I have found many young adults long for guidance from trustworthy older saints who don't offer bumper sticker clichés but instead provide hard-earned wisdom. In this wonderfully practical yet richly theological work, we have honest and relevant reflections offered to the next generation of believers. Whether struggling with questions about doubt or vocation, sex or suffering, this book does not shy away from real challenges. I encourage young and old to read these pages; we can all learn from the balanced vision it provides."

Kelly M. Kapic, professor of theological studies at Covenant College

"This book addresses some of the most important questions my students ask me both in class and in our individual conversations, speaking to the ways that Christian education at its best impacts students' daily lives and not just their academic knowledge. I look forward to offering this book as a resource to my students."

Mary Veeneman, professor of biblical and theological Studies at North Park University

Life
Questions
Every
Student
Asks

FAITHFUL RESPONSES
TO COMMON ISSUES

Edited by
Gary M. Burge *and*
David Lauber

IVP
Academic
An imprint of InterVarsity Press
Downers Grove, Illinois

InterVarsity Press
P.O. Box 1400, Downers Grove, IL 60515-1426
ivpress.com
email@ivpress.com

InterVarsity Press® is the book-publishing division of InterVarsity Christian Fellowship/USA®, a movement of
students and faculty active on campus at hundreds of universities, colleges, and schools of nursing in the United
States of America, and a member movement of the International Fellowship of Evangelical Students. For
information about local and regional activities, visit intervarsity.org.

All Scripture quotations, unless otherwise indicated, are taken from The Holy Bible, New International Version®,
NIV®. Copyright © 1973, 1978, 1984, 2011 by Biblica, Inc.™ Used by permission of Zondervan. All rights reserved
worldwide. www.zondervan.com. The "NIV" and "New International Version" are trademarks registered in the
United States Patent and Trademark Office by Biblica, Inc.™

While any stories in this book are true, some names and identifying information may have been changed to protect
the privacy of individuals.

Cover design and image composite: Beth McGill
Interior design: Daniel van Loon
Images: student legs © PeopleImages / E+ / Getty Images

ISBN 978-0-8308-5332-8 (print)
ISBN 978-0-8308-5333-5 (digital)

Printed in the United States of America ∞

Library of Congress Cataloging-in-Publication Data
A catalog record for this book is available from the Library of Congress.

P	25	24	23	22	21	20	19	18	17	16	15	14	13	12	11	10	9	8	7	6	5	4	3	2	1
Y	37	36	35	34	33	32	31	30	29	28	27	26	25	24	23	22	21	20							

Contents

Foreword

SO, YOU'VE PICKED UP THIS BOOK. Maybe it was given to you by a pastor or even assigned to you by a teacher to read.

You're curious or maybe even skeptical: "Does the church really have an answer to *this*?"

- You spent a semester abroad and were exposed to poverty in a way that shook you. How should you think about wealth and power now? How should you actively promote justice and mercy where you are now?

- You attended the funeral of a classmate who died of cancer. You watch friends deal with mental health challenges and fears of the future. Another friend has a mom with dementia. Where is God in all of this?

- Visiting churches is hard. Where to park, where to go in, where to sit? Did I dress right? Do I like this space? The music? The preaching? Is this even worth it? Why do we have to go to church anyway?

- Everyone my age is dating. Or at least it seems like it. Is there a Christian way to date or to think about marriage? Is it okay to stay single? Are some people "called" to marriage or singleness?

- What's with that idea of calling? If I just take classes I enjoy or pursue something that will guarantee me a job, is that good enough?

- And what if I find this whole Christianity thing hard to take? What if I doubt these things I've been taught? Is it sinful to doubt?

If you haven't asked these questions, you probably have friends who have. If you've had these questions, maybe you've never said anything to anyone and you're struggling. Or maybe you haven't known who to ask.

So, you may be wondering: Does the church have something to say about the questions lodged deep in my heart? Can I have conversations about the things that matter most?

Yes.

This book is an invitation. Here your older siblings are asking and then—gently, prayerfully, seriously—answering the very questions you want answered. Will you always agree with the answers? Maybe not. But you will find their writing Christ-centered, biblical, and wise. The authors are people who know and love college students. They write with the compassion of older siblings and the intelligence and warmth of your favorite professors. Their words are insightful, personal, and humble.

So, go ahead. Get to it. Wrestle with some of the most challenging questions of our faith, and do it with people who've been thinking about these things for a long time. You are not alone. You've got people.

Jesus was known as someone who asked and answered a lot of good questions. May you sense his love and guidance as you ask and seek answers for some of your own.

Mary S. Hulst
University Pastor, Calvin University

Contributors

Gary M. Burge, PhD, dean of the faculty and professor of New Testament, Calvin Theological Seminary

David B. Capes, PhD, senior research scholar, Lanier Theological Library

Elisha Eveleigh, PhD, pediatric psychologist, Dayton Children's Hospital

James G. Huff Jr., PhD, associate professor of HNGR (Human Needs and Global Resources) and anthropology, and associate director of HNGR, Wheaton College

Mary S. Hulst, PhD, university pastor, Calvin University

Keith L. Johnson, PhD, professor of theology, Wheaton College

Beth Felker Jones, PhD, professor of theology, Wheaton College

David Lauber, PhD, dean of the school of biblical and theological studies and associate professor of theology, Wheaton College

Emily Hunter McGowin, PhD, assistant professor of theology, Wheaton College

Benjamin Norquist, MA, managing director of the Wheaton Center for Faith & Innovation, Wheaton College

Amy Peeler, PhD, associate professor of New Testament, Wheaton College

Margaret Kim Peterson, PhD, fellow, Chicago Center for Family Health

Matt Vega, MA, PhD candidate, University of Chicago

Preface

GARY M. BURGE AND DAVID LAUBER

THE JOB OF A PROFESSOR OFTEN CONSISTS of things you'd never expect. We prepare lectures and deliver them. We manage long lists of students and their grades. And we attend meetings—lots of meetings. However, one feature few know about are the many private conversations faculty have with students. These take place over lunch, during office hours, or even casually when walking across the campus. The alert professor realizes that these are not merely casual conversations but are moments when students ask their most profound questions about their faith, their lives, and their futures. They are sacred conversations because many of their themes live close to the heart where pain is hidden, confusion lurks, and happiness is trying to make a breakthrough. We are all like the young girl named Riley in Pixar's film *Inside Out* (2015) where joy, sadness, anger, fear, and disgust are struggling for control of Riley's inner control panel.

We take these conversations very seriously because we are committed to our students' well-being. We really do care. We recognize that our students are whole people and not simply members of a class. They are growing, struggling, questioning, and wondering about the large issues of life as young adults. And so we listen intently to their questions and concerns, and we seek to provide wise counsel and direction. Often, we leave these conversations with a prayer that what we discussed has been helpful and life-giving.

Frequently we find ourselves drawing upon the material we have worked through in class. And when we are alone, we may be able to make connections to the personal and existential questions that each student carries. It is one thing to talk about a biblical and theological account of suffering in a theology class and another thing to help a student make sense of the recent suicide of one of their high school friends. It is one thing to work out the moral and theological meaning of marriage but quite another to wonder about a divorce that is working its way through a student's family.

There are also other timeless questions that we hear again and again. How do we discover our vocation? How do we find a sustained community when we leave college? What is the value of church (when I really don't want to go)? What about doubt or suffering? And what do we make of our neighbors who are Muslims, and yet we like and respect them deeply? We may even admire their spirituality. Can they teach us anything about God?

This book represents twelve conversations we have had with students throughout our careers. If we were asked to distill the big themes we have heard again and again, themes that resonate with students throughout our country, most would be located in this list.

This book is a companion to our *Theology Questions Everyone Asks: Christian Faith in Plain Language.*[1] That book is intended as a supplement to theology textbooks or surveys of Christian thought. It is a supplement in that it takes up contemporary questions students frequently ask in class as they work through classic theological doctrines. The questions addressed with thoughtful biblical and theological answers were intended to inspire reflection, and even disagreement, but most of all, serious and mature engagement.

This companion volume moves from theoretical classroom questions to practical life-defining questions. In our first book we pursued a close and careful reading of Scripture and carefully nuanced theological judgments in order to give guidance to some of theology's most difficult questions. Here, once again, we reach for the Bible and the wisdom of the church—joined with many years of fruitful teaching and men-toring—to provide a different sort of guidance.

The answers to these personal questions belong to each writer of each chapter. They do not belong to the institutions represented by each individual author; nor does one set of answers reflect how another scholar, teacher, or practitioner might approach such questions. Simply put, we are thinking aloud with the wider community of teachers and students, exploring how urgent and weighty personal questions might find faithful and creative answers.

While we wrote these chapters with students in mind, we recognize that we have much to learn from each other as well. As professors, we have heard variations of the same questions in our conversations with individual students over the years. Reading the thoughtful and com-pelling answers of our colleagues will no doubt provide us with greater resources for future conversations during office hours or over a meal or cup of coffee. Our hope is that college teachers, chaplains, and pastors will benefit just as we have from listening in on the wise and faithful guidance given by our colleagues to the pressing questions we hear from college students year after year.

Chapter One

Community and Friendship

GARY M. BURGE

FOR THE LAST TWELVE MONTHS, I've been engaged in a form of crisis intervention that I didn't see coming. It is a long-distance conversation with one of my favorite students (I'll call her Beth) who graduated from Wheaton College a few years ago.[1] Beth was a gifted leader in her class, a sit-in-the-front-row student, an inspiration for her peers, active leading dorm Bible study groups, and a poster child for the admissions office. You know the type. She was even humble about all her achievements, which only made her more impressive. While Beth was at Wheaton, we met often and in some odd way, our relationship morphed from that of a student-professor to something else. A friendship perhaps within the peculiar confines of those limited college years on campus. I'm glad we kept up because now our emails have a foundation of hours upon hours of relationship building that came years before. Both of us are honest and tough in what we say. It's the honesty part that makes me respect her as much as I do.

But Beth is in a crisis. Career dreams didn't work out after graduation. She isn't certain about graduate school and is wise not to enroll someplace just because she needs a place to go. She moved to the city where she'd grown up, but now most of her friends are gone. The guy she thought would be "the one" disappeared sometime in the winter of her senior year. She's back in her high school bedroom living with her parents who are desperately trying to remember that she's no longer sixteen. And—this is the surprising part—she announced to me this year that she is officially abandoning her Christian faith: "It simply doesn't give me a satisfying worldview any longer." She is looking now for a job, and I think she has two criteria: how much money she can make and how quickly she can move out. It all makes me wish we were back on campus together, having lunch in Wheaton's Anderson Commons and having a fiercely honest conversation like we used to do.

The one common thread in her life—the one constant I've seen since she was a sophomore and I now know reaches back to high school—is that she was the runner who ran alone. Beth likes going fast and far, and she's competitive. She often crosses every finish line first and alone. And while she collects more trophies and is cheered relentlessly, now the cheering seems muted, the trophies are boxed up someplace, and she sits in the corner of a Starbucks and gets depressed. *This is the nightmare scenario that many of my students secretly worry about.* Solitary. Filled with self-doubt. Poor. Afraid. Cheerfully working at Forever Twenty-One and hating it.

There are a lot of topics on the table here: vocational discernment, isolation, self-care, poor preparation for life after graduation, and questions about faith. And each of them is legitimate and worthy of long discussion. But these require triage because the truth is, Beth is falling apart. And has been for months.

"Are you surrounded by any sort of community that knows you and loves you—and can speak truthfully into your life?" I ask. That sort of question would be natural on a college campus where we are surrounded by innumerable opportunities for community building inside the dorm, in student development events, athletic programs, chapel, even classroom friendships. But once we graduate, as one student told me, it is like leaving the forest and entering the desert. Which is only partially true. Communities can be built anyplace with the right effort.

But Beth was at a loss. "I found this group that meets at a guy's house. Most are lapsed evangelicals or post-Christian, and it's pretty cynical. And we drink a lot." That's what I mean about honesty. "Is it a community for you?" "Hardly."

THE SIGNIFICANCE OF COMMUNITY

When we are not connected to a genuine community, we are fragile and vulnerable. If we fall, there is no net. One of the central facts about us as persons is that we need each other. We are social beings. An assured result of social science research over the last seventy-five years is that we do need each other and that people who live in isolation begin to languish. This is not only true of newborn babies who may be abandoned to a crib for hours on end but also of the elderly for whom isolation is a critical component of their well-being. Careful psychological study has been done since the 1950s on the solitary confinement of prisoners as a form of punishment. Their cell is 80 square feet, smaller than a horse stall. Researchers now consider it cruel and have shown that it creates profound psychological damage. Severe isolation eventually kills us.

But we do not need researchers to tell us this. I imagine that instinctively we know this to be self-evident. We know the desire we had in early school years to fit in. We remember the mild trauma of entering a cafeteria and anxiously hoping someone will wave and call us to a table. We know the desire we had in high school to belong to some team, club, or organization (even if it's only the prom planning committee)—a tribe really—that meant we belong to something beyond ourselves. Where our name is known. That if we didn't show up, someone might notice. That if we were sad, someone would care. And that if we had really good news, someone might want to hear it. That desire for human connection and support, for belonging and shared identity is so close to our hearts it can barely be measured. This reflex to some degree explains the rise of social networking (Facebook, Instagram, etc.) where we invite "friends" to join a networked "community." Of course, many have asked just what sort of community this really is. It's a fair question.

I remember leading a small seminar with about twenty students a few years ago. We were close and knew each other well. We were all in class one day with the exception of a guy who viewed himself (I guessed) as living on the margin. "Where is Daniel?" I asked. "Dining hall" they answered because they'd seen him there. So I asked if anybody had his cell number. Someone did. And we shared it, and twenty texts hit his phone at once: "We miss you and can't start without you." He sprinted to the class, burst in, the class cheered, and we were underway. And it said to everyone there—not just one young man—that we care and you matter. He never forgot this and liked to tell the story laughing. He was no longer on the margin.

This instinctive desire for belonging is why societies throughout the world have built and sustained social structures and networks that give meaning and resilience to life. Good marriages, families, neighborhoods, schools, churches, and jobs each must have some component of community in them, or else, they fail in what we need most. We want to belong. We want to have membership. We want others to recognize that our being there matters. Even advertisers know this. Today they don't simply sell you a product; they sell you an identity and membership. Subaru owners aren't consumers, they belong to *the Subaru family*, which explains why they have owner rallies and events, which (oddly in my mind) gather up thousands of people whose only link is their car. In 2018, eighty-four hundred such people showed up in Stafford Springs, Connecticut, for Subaru's "Wicked Big Event." It is fascinating to wonder what they were seeking. Last week, I saw a billboard fifty miles west of Detroit. "Love is out there . . ." "Find it in a new Subaru Crosstrek." I'm confident most of us are looking for a different sort of love.

On the flip side, no doubt for many of us, by the time we enter adulthood, we have seen innumerable failed communities, friendship betrayals, disloyalties, and disappointments. I have known many students who have come from deeply broken families where the absence of affection and belonging had been damaging to them. And I've known many students who thought they were in a community at school but then experienced rejection or judgment, and this had crippling effects on their life. These adults were entering life in their twenties wary and cautious about risking the vulnerability that could come with joining another community or relationship again. "When you've been hurt enough times, why set yourself up for it again?" is what one student told me. But our need often outweighs our logic. Our yearning for community makes us try once more. Only in the most tragic cases do a few people decide that a solitary life is going to be their destiny, and so they stop trying altogether. I knew someone in his early thirties who was utterly attached to his dog. It was obvious in how they lived together, almost like roommates. "You two are really close," I said. My friend responded, "You really can't count on people, but this guy, well, he's always there for you." I was amazed and frankly saddened. But I understood.

CHRISTIAN COMMUNITY

The classic and time-honored treatment of the importance of community was written in 1938 by Dietrich Bonhoeffer, a German pastor, who titled his book *Gemeinsames Leben* (the common life or shared life). It was translated in 1954 as *Life Together*. Bonhoeffer was a pastor during the troubling years of Hitler's reign. He joined the Confessing Church (that resisted Nazi nationalism) and took charge of a clandestine seminary for training young pastors. *Life Together* is Bonhoeffer's description of what it means to live in community. During this time he also published *Nachfolge* (imitation [of Christ]), which was translated into English as *The Cost of Discipleship*. These two books are timeless treatments that every Christian should know and cherish. For his efforts, Bonhoeffer was arrested by the Gestapo in 1943, sent to prison, and two years later on April 9, 1945, martyred at Flossenbürg concentration camp as the Nazi regime was unraveling.

Bonhoeffer's first words to us in *Life Together* come from Scripture: "How good and pleasant it is when God's people live together in unity" (Ps 133:1). He could have continued:

It is like precious oil poured on the head,
    running down on the beard,
running down on Aaron's beard,
    down on the collar of his robe.

It is as if the dew of Hermon
  were falling on Mount Zion.
For there the LORD bestows his blessing,
  even life forevermore. (Psalm 133:2-3)

What does it mean in these verses when it says: *For there the Lord bestows his blessing*? Where is "there?" What is this location where goodness and blessing enrich us, where we experience unity and belonging and meaning? For Bonhoeffer (and countless other writers) these words describe what should be a precious reality about the gathered community of the church. It should be a place, as Bonhoeffer wrote, "of incomparable joy and strength" for each of us.[2] But go slowly here. The church *may be* that building you visit once a week. But not necessarily. The church is in its simplest terms the gathering of Jesus' disciples who come together to love, strengthen, and support one another in the context of gospel and sacrament. The church is simply a community that desires to worship God and develop a clear understanding of the kingdom of Christ and the kingdoms of this world.

But we learn in *Life Together* that this sort of community is a hard-won reality. Certainly, in 1940s Germany it was. We read about its ideals throughout the New Testament. In books like Ephesians we are offered a lofty promise that the "boundless riches of Christ" can be uncovered here (Eph 3:8), where our gifts are discovered and celebrated (Eph 4:11), and where an invested community speaks "truth in love" so that we mature and deepen our knowledge of love (Eph 4:15-16). In books like Philippians we read about Paul's vision for how a well-knit community can be a place where we genuinely stand up for each other, where fear is banished, and friendship-destroying competition disappears (Phil 1:27-30). Even in Jesus' final days his mind was on this church, and he prays that it will become a place that is life-giving and faithful not just to him but to its fellow members (Jn 17:1-19; cf. Jn 13:34-35).

Therefore, the first thing we need to grasp is that we *must* belong to a sustainable community of fellow believers. This can only be life-giving when (as Bonhoeffer says) the gathering is centered on Jesus and his grace. The more profoundly we have experienced God's grace and love, the more profoundly we will be able to extend those gifts to others (Rom 15:7). When we have received God's mercy, then we become merciful. This, Bonhoeffer says, is the foundation. When communities come together in weakness—having received forgiveness and grace—then competition, judgment, accusation, and anger recede. This then forms a community unlike anything in the world; it is a divine or spiritual community where uncanny experiences of love erupt. Posturing and image management—those deadly toxins that seem to be everywhere—can now be set aside. And truth, centered now not on the whims of the society around us, but truth taken from the Scriptures and the great saints who have preceded us, centers and define us.

THE CHURCH

Of course, this is the ideal profile of the church. In every respect it ought to be that place where truth is announced in an understandable way, where lives are changed, where deep friendship is celebrated, and where hospitality is common. Where we can bring our friend and not have to code-switch when we're there. Where the meaning of the Sunday morning isn't defined by three hymns, a prayer, an offering, and a three-point sermon. Nor, for that matter, where another liturgy gives just a newer formula: a hymn set with a band, awesome screen graphics, and a funny and urgent message with a guy sporting a soul patch and a black T-shirt.

Neither of these formulas is really what we're seeking. One may be more entertaining than the other, but they are not a guarantee of anything that will meet our deepest need. When we probe beneath the surface, we may discover that the deeper values we desire are not there. In traditional churches we see formal structures that were established long before we were born. We may hear music that may have the feel of religion from a distant generation. It seems that there is a social organization swirling around the place, but we wonder how or if we can fit in. Or we might decide we do not want to fit in. Few seek us out and fewer still know what to do with us. Sometimes the church can miss the mark of becoming a community. So our aim is not necessarily to join a church but to join a Christian community—and I hope that this is a church that knows how to weave the fabric of community into its life and make us a part of it.

Here in my city (Grand Rapids, Michigan) there are two churches I find intriguing. I know their pastors, and I know their mission. They are aiming at an audience in their twenties or thirties who they claim are postchurch. These are young adults who grew up in church, understand its culture, but quit attending after they left high school. And they swore they never would go back. When the Local Church and Encounter Church began, they were not freewheeling startups. They were led by mature young pastors anchored to other mature congregations. But the key was they knew that something had to change; something was missing, and so they needed to build a community differently. On the first anniversary of the Local Church in 2018, they already had over two hundred postchurch young adults attending regularly.

I wonder how many times I have had conversations with twenty-something adults who tell me that they have given up on church. In their minds they either have a memory of a childhood relic, or they have had some sour experience of attending a church they thought was meaningless. However, in every city—and this is a guarantee—there are fantastic examples of churches where community is alive and well, where the music makes sense, where the message is relevant, and where people will eagerly welcome us and find a place for us to be who we truly are. The question is never whether they exist; the question is, Are we willing to do the work required to locate them and try once more?

This is vital because when I am in a genuinely Christian community, I am mysteriously strengthened. This kind of community helps me build a sustainable life in a very difficult world. Bonhoeffer famously wrote in *Life Together*, we need each other because *the Christ in the heart of a fellow believer is always stronger than the Christ in my own heart*.[3] I need to be someplace where, when I am at my lowest, there are others who are willing to help lift me up. Or when I am confused, I am with mature Christians who can help keep me from becoming my own worst enemy. And when I am desperate and anxious, I have a phone number, someone who will listen and interpret my circumstances with wisdom, experience, and spiritual maturity. And if need be, simply come over.

But such community experiences are not one-way streets. We are not only received and cared for, but there is genuine reciprocity and we understand that listening, lifting up others, guiding the lost, and providing wisdom are our assignments too. If we step into a community and only come to take its resources, we will deplete it rather than grow it. It is no different than a friendship: if there is no reciprocity, no giving (as well as taking), then that friendship will begin to wither and die.

This is precisely what my friend Beth does not have. She went to church dutifully while she was in college, but it was not a real community to her. She did not explore, nor did she invest the effort. On her church scorecard she got all the best marks—she joined a recognized, established, respected, tall brick church brimming with successful adults— but sadly it had become nothing but a lonely experience for her. And someplace in her soul, she stopped believing in the church or in Christian community. She stopped looking, and she stopped hoping. And soon this spiritual despair bled over to her other less formal friendships. She didn't invest, and she didn't expect more from them. She evolved into a person having a solitary life, and she lost the skills (and desire) to pursue community. And she did this when she was surrounded by opportunities and other young adults who wanted the same thing. But when she left college, when she was on her own, when she entered a distant city, she didn't know what it meant to have a trusted friend, much less a trusted community. When she was collapsing, she didn't have a single valuable phone number to call except for her mom's.

INTENTIONALITY, FRIENDSHIP, AND COMMUNITY

One of our problems is that we often sit back and wait for community to find us. Or we think that finding such a community will be an easy task. But both of these ideas are wrongheaded. We need to be intentional about finding a Christian community, and we need to acknowledge that this will take work. It is the same when we wonder why we have so few friends when essentially, we are waiting for someone to reach out to us. Friendship often requires us to initiate a relationship, which then grows into something meaningful.

So in our diminishing hope, where do we begin? Perhaps something even more basic, more elementary, needs to be on our assignment list. We need to discover how to grow a fledgling community right where we are. And this may simply begin with friendship. We know we need understanding, compassion, support, and accountability. And sometimes the best place to start is with one friend, someone who can be trusted, someone with whom we can build something we've not had before. A friend where intimacy and deep knowing are possible. Imagine. Imagine having someone with whom you're not competitive or fearful, someone who will protect you from those who would harm you, someone who might love you in the sense that David loved Jonathan. Imagine. Imagine finding someone whose value to you isn't in their social status, their career potential, their beauty, or the social power they possess. Not in the things the world finds attractive or compelling. These are superficialities, and you know this already. But this is someone you find whose qualities are profound: grace, forgiveness, charity, hopefulness, trustworthiness, and love. You already know the mechanics of friendship pursuits that are empty and vain. You've known this since high school. You watched *Mean Girls*. This is something different, and this friend will likely have attributes that are rare but to be treasured.

I have known many, many students who have taken this charge of friendship and community building seriously. And by their senior year at college, they have built something remarkable. I have seen small groups of men and women who have decided to be lifelong friends, and by their senior year they live together. I've been in these homes and shared meals with these students and seen the community they are building. It is inspiring. They share meals, chores, and a vision for what their life will become. And here is the best part—they make a vow that they will stick with each other for the rest of their lives. I have seen them return for reunions. I have heard about their annual plans to fly to a common city for a weekend, stay in a great hotel, and spend two days catching up. I know they build private social media channels (like a private Facebook page) to talk regularly. One group has a private online Word Press diary they keep, and each one writes in it weekly. But the key is that they have built friendships that have become old friendships, and these have evolved into a community that now sustains them. They show up at each other's weddings. And when they have their children, I know they are there for each other. I've seen them appear when their children get baptized. And when one of their parents dies, they do not miss the funeral. These are the people who show up in our life. And when inevitable tragedy strikes, they will be at our side. My wife has such a friend from college. Her husband died from a heart attack in his late forties. We attended his funeral, and there I saw faces and names that reached back decades. They showed up.

It is never too late to begin this process. It is so easy to think, *But this didn't come together for me when I was in college. I was left behind, or no one really wanted me to join their private exclusive group.* But here is a secret whose importance I can barely measure. *The challenge of building community will stay with you for the rest of your life. And it can begin at any time.* You may move and find yourself in a new city. You may experience major life changes. And you will have to begin anew. And beginning with friendship that expands to community will once again be necessary work. In 2017, I moved from Wheaton College near Chicago (after twenty-five years) and joined the faculty of Calvin Theological Seminary in Grand Rapids, Michigan. Our best friends in Wheaton remain good friends, but we knew we had to begin this process once more. I was alert to the possibility of new friendships, and God opened a beautiful door. An economics professor at Calvin University became a friend. He is a trustworthy person who understands what friendship means. One afternoon, he even hosted a gathering of eight Calvin faculty at a nearby pub just so I could meet more people. And as our friendship matured, our wives came to know each other, and this led to an invitation to visit their church, which led to us joining their house group. Today, we have found a healthy church, a good community, and after a major life transition, we are not alone. We know people who show up for each other. And I know they'll eventually show up for us.

Beth needs to stop waiting for community to find her and launch out with all the imagination and ingenuity that I know she has. She needs to assess where friendship might be found. She needs to do the hard work of searching out the churches and communities where her peer group can be discovered so that friendships can be born and deepen and possibly emerge into genuine communities for her. And the church could be a part of this plan. I don't believe she has rejected the Christian faith completely. I believe she has rejected one form of it that she now views as rigid and compromised. And the happy discovery for her will be finding a church that is utterly unlike that place she once called church. Beth is now postchurch, but she doesn't know yet that there are thousands of millennials just like her who are seeking something new.

But Beth's greatest challenge will be her willingness to try. To hope and believe that there are other adults just like her who want to be in a trusted friendship that gives birth to community.

FEATURES OF COMMUNITY

Christine Pohl is a professor of ethics at a seminary in Kentucky. Her recent book, *Living into Community: Cultivating Practices That Sustain Us* has been a helpful guide to many of us who are trying to sort out what a genuine community is supposed to look like.[4] Her work on community has been a twenty-year project that first appeared in her book *Making Room: Recovering Hospitality as s Christian Tradition* (1999).[5] Then a few years ago, thanks to a major grant, Pohl began a more comprehensive research project to study the characteristics of sustainable communities that genuinely give life to their members. She organized a prolonged consultation with a large group of pastors, community leaders, and professors, and gleaned from these meetings (and many readings) the features of healthy communities. She prefers to avoid abstraction in this effort and wants to see what real living, breathing people do when they build this sort of life for themselves.

Four themes emerged throughout her work and these have now become classic discussion starters for those who wonder if they belong to a community. At least they are high virtues that provide aspirational goals for each of us: gratitude, promise keeping, truth giving, and hospitality. Let's look at each of these briefly.

1. *Gratitude*. Pohl teaches us that gratitude has always been basic to the Christian faith because it connects with our experience of grace. When we see more of life as gift (and less as entitlement) we begin to see things differently.

However, she is clear that there are new skills we must acquire if we build this sort of community. This living requires concentration. We must work hard to notice, to remember what we see, and to speak to the person who deserves recognition. It then becomes a way of life that may be contagious if shared among many. But remarkably, gratitude is also an act of resistance against habits that permeate our world: cynicism, envy, criticism, and negativity. As a relational practice, it builds up all those it touches.

2. *Promise keeping*. Here Pohl teaches us that the great deformation of most of our relationships is betrayal. When we betray someone, we choose self-interest over the longevity of faithfulness to others. In this community virtue, we choose to become dependable, establish trust, and invest in our futures together because without reliable promises, there can be no future.

This evokes memories of what we were taught as children about "keeping your promise." This is not something we measure by single instances of faithfulness. This is about cultivating a life known by its loyalty and reliability, whose dependability is predictable. We become promise-keeping people. To love someone takes on value when it occurs over many, many years and when circumstances are either difficult or ordinary. But this too is an act of resistance today. Our world tells us to keep our options open in case something better comes along. And we are to have a sensible degree of cautious distrust because, well, not everyone is going to reciprocate our faithfulness. Promise keeping says *no* to all this. It builds grounded and stable relationships.

3. Truth giving. Pohl says that a routine deformation of our relationships is deception. We do not tell the truth, or more bluntly we lie. In one sense, truth giving is related to promise giving since it speaks to our need to be faithful and honest with those we live with. Lying, on the other hand, erodes trust. But this is also related to gratitude because gratefulness eliminates the need for posturing and image management and can lead to honesty.

The Quaker tradition made truthfulness one of its most important virtues. Their outline: (1) Listen "for the truth in the words of others"; (2) speak the truth as you understand it with "cordiality, kindness and love"; (3) avoid "gossip, tale-bearing, breaking confidences, or the disparagement of others"; and (4) resist "temptations to falsehood, coercion, and abuse." Pohl concludes, "adopting these commitments would transform many of our . . . families and congregations."[6]

4. Hospitality. Last, we learn that hospitality grows out of gratitude as well. We rejoice in what we have, and we choose to share *particularly* with the stranger. The Greek word for hospitality is *philoxenia* or "love of the stranger." In this sense hospitality cultivates a sacrificial lifestyle that gives more than it takes because we have been given already so much. We don't live with a worldview of scarcity but abundance and believe much can be distributed. However, this sharing is most often centered on time. We spend time with each other (which is also a resource), and this means we are sharing life with each other.

Someone once said that a good community is like a good hotel: it anticipates your needs and yet recognizes its own boundaries and limits. It is perceptive of what is needed and patient with those who are vulnerable. Its measure is found in the welcome it extends to those who desperately need one.

Pohl believes that together these four attributes are commonplace in healthy communities. But they can also be the aspirations of communities (and friendships) that want to grow into something better. Who wouldn't want to live a life supported and fed by such a community as this? Who wouldn't want to be known as a builder who contributes to making something that seems so foreign in today's world?

FINAL ADVICE FOR BETH

I often find myself imagining the most honest email I could ever send to Beth. What would I say that wed truth and grace? That held both challenge and generosity of spirit? That was honest and yet did not push her away?

> Dear Beth:
>
> I am so grateful for you and our many-year friendship. I have known you since you were about nineteen, and with each passing year I have admired your gifts, your passion, and your honesty with me. Today you are forging adult patterns in life that will stay with you for decades. Since you were a child, you were sustained by a family that loved you and schools that provided you with countless programs that kept you busy, so busy that I wonder if you ever stopped to see what you really loved, what mattered, or how this busy-ness was changing you.
>
> But now things are different. I can hear in your writing pain and desperation that I have never heard before. It is in circumstances like this when everything purposeful seems to have disappeared that we discover what is truly inside of us. But it is also a time to take stock and possibly rebuild; to start over or take advantage of what's around you.
>
> Can I take a risk with you? You are someone who likes to achieve things, and the list of achievements on your résumé (thanks for sending it!) is truly astounding. These are remarkable accomplishments that few at twenty-five would ever complete. I'm proud of you.
>
> As I look back over my many years with college students, I think I've discovered something I wish I'd known when I was twenty-five. The secret to sustained happiness and personal fulfillment isn't found in what we do as it is found in who we do it with. Climbing Everest is great; climbing Everest with six lifelong friends is better. Someday when you can no longer climb, you'll have a shared experience together you'll draw

on for years. And these six may become profound friends who will always be there for each other.

But you never learned this secret. Sometimes adults enjoy a student's successes and don't want to end the parade of trophies. Sometimes they are fearful that if you reject their advice you'll also reject them. So I am going to take a risk. Beth, the solution here isn't in further striving, another opportunity, one more brilliant job well done. It won't be found in that grad school you're dreaming about and what a new shiny MA might look like. You have enough trophies.

You need to stop and find a friend. And through that friend begin to find a community that will sustain you. Where honesty, trust, generosity, and hopefulness are shared. My own hope is that this community is formed by those who follow Jesus. I know I'm repeating myself, but I'll say it again. What you thought was Christian community in your many years in church was a vague and empty semblance of the real thing. A seed of cynicism was planted in you (at church? in college?), and it is growing. It will consume you eventually, and before long you'll be hosting those drinking parties you now attend (and do not admire). Do not lose hope. You know how to work hard against long odds. You can do this too. God has been enormously good to you. Begin with thankfulness that he has given you what you need to do this. When we surround ourselves with a genuine community, our life can be redirected, things can be put in perspective, and new thinking emerge. And who knows, you may become the one healed who ends up healing others.

Let's talk about next steps. Who is the most trusted person you know? And what are your options for locating the best possible community in your city? I think that God has a new fantastic chapter to write in your life. And what's in it are things that will utterly surprise you. You'll have to pull together a lot of courage to join this new story, but I can tell you one thing with confidence, if you want to, you'll be able to do it.

Chapter Two

Vocation

BEN NORQUIST

How can my life count for something? What should I do with my life? Will I lead a happy life? What good work am I called to?

If these questions were people, we might not like them all the time. They would be the kinds of people who make us feel uncomfortable at times, who put us out of our comfort zones. Their honesty about our personal limitations and failings might seem rude. But on the other hand, they would be the kind of people who help us grow and learn new things, who help us be better versions of ourselves, and who help us clarify our own values. Hanging out with them would make us better people.

We often think of these questions as dominating our college years, but in my experience they actually remain with us throughout life. Although you might focus on these questions now, you won't answer them in any final way—spending time with these questions will be a life's work. They evolve and mature as years pass, and we will continue to circle back to them as we enter and pass through new life stages. Perhaps you can think of these questions as traveling companions with whom you will have a lifelong relationship, and as you grow and age, so will they. Reflecting on them provides an important foundation for a whole host of decisions you'll make throughout life—decisions about relationships, where to live, what work to pursue, how to spend your time, and so on. These are some of the most pressing questions we will face in life. Let's think about them together for a few minutes.

DEFINING VOCATION

There are countless secular ideas about work and calling. As Christians in the Western world, we tend to conflate our callings with our careers. When you turned to this chapter, you might have thought, *Oh, this is the chapter about discerning what career path to choose.* But *vocation* is not quite the same as *career.* The word *vocation* carries deeper, richer, more communal, and even more spiritual connotations than the term *career.* Your career is simply the course of your life's paid work—it is a sequence of jobs. Your vocation, on the other hand, defines deeper layers of meaning and purpose in your life. It is about what you give the greatest commitments and energies of your life to. Can a career or a job be a context for a vocation? Yes, they can be. But they are not the same thing.

In the West, we also tend to love what a friend of mine calls the "passion hypothesis" about our vocations—the idea that the secret to happiness is following our dreams and that this will lead us to our true calling. This thesis plays a central role in many of our favorite movies and stories. Unfortunately, this value for "following your passion" underpins contemporary Christian books about calling, as well. However, it's not very biblical in the long run. Deconstructing the passion hypothesis and other misleading ideas about calling and rebuilding our approach in a redemptive way is difficult work, but it is also rewarding and can become an important dimension of our Christian discipleship.

Trying to define the word *calling* can be tricky business when cultural ideas like the passion hypothesis exercise such a strong grip on our imaginations. The good news is that as Christians we benefit from biblical revelation and thousands of years of Judeo-Christian reflection about vocation and calling (the terms *calling* and *vocation* can be thought of as synonyms, so I will use them interchangeably throughout this chapter). As Christians, we are members of a tradition that has thought long and hard about good work and life well-lived. Although the idea of calling has meant different things at different times, drawing on the insight of our tradition, there are at least three distinctive senses I'll point out:

1. *Vocation as a general, shared role or responsibility.* God calls us all to the Christian life, to follow Jesus, to love God and neighbor, to forgive our enemies, and so on. This vocation is not a calling that's for some Christians and not for others—it is our shared calling. This is what the Puritans called our "general calling."[1]

2. *Vocation as a matter of personal discretion, guided by the Holy Spirit and by wisdom.* In this sense, calling is something that emerges as we make decisions about where we can apply our skills and passions to address some need in the world. This is something akin to what the Puritans referred to as our "particular callings."

3. *Vocation as a mystical experience, a particular and specific communication from God to perform a task or take on a role.* Moses, called to free the Hebrews from Egypt, is a good example, or think about Mary, specially called to be the mother of Jesus—miraculously. Most of us won't receive this kind of calling—these miracles were restricted to special circumstances in the Bible and are probably uncommon today as well (though they still occur and we should always be ready to hear from God however he chooses to communicate with us).

If you look closely, *calling* turns out to have multiple parts: *a caller who calls, our response to the calling,* and *a community that benefits from our calling.* First of all, there is a caller. Callings come *from someone.* Christians believe that they come from God. Second, callings are invitations to some kind of response on our part. These responses might be to give effort toward some task, make a sacrifice of some kind, dedicate our energy in a long-term direction, invest in a relationship, or to respond in some other way. Third, callings are in service to others. In my roles as a son to my parents, brother to my siblings, father to my children, and husband to my wife, I have callings to love and care for them. They are the beneficiaries of my callings, and I am the beneficiary of their callings, which means they suffer when I neglect my vocations. So, there is always a community of some kind within which our callings are lived out, indeed, *for which* they are lived out. Another way to think about it is that callings are (1) from God, (2) to people, (3) for the sake of others.

Thinking about vocation in this way bears some good fruit. If callings are from God to people for others, calling has both its *origin* and its *purpose* outside of us. This way of thinking about vocation also provides significant encouragement for those of us who struggle with feelings of inferiority—it makes us an irreplaceable part of our calling. We are equipped with moral power and the ability to accept and fulfill the responsibilities God gives us. Just remember, God doesn't give us responsibilities without giving us what we need to fulfill them (2 Pet 1:3). Finally, thinking about vocation in these relational terms emphasizes that our callings are rich ways that we fulfill the greatest commandments: to love God and our neighbors.

Notice also that thinking about vocation in this way significantly leaves out several points. There is no mention of personal passions, so it leaves room for callings to unwanted tasks (look to Moses's calling for a biblical example or the many ways in which we carry responsibilities that don't align with our passions today). It also doesn't mention the level of difficulty or sacrifice, leaving room for callings to easy tasks as well as toilsome work. Finally, this way of thinking about vocation doesn't refer to personal strengths and weaknesses, thus leaving room for reliance on others and indeed on the power of God in the practice of our vocations.

Does God still miraculously call specific people to specific tasks (like the callings he gave to Moses and Mary)? I think he does, but it may not be very common—it wasn't common in the time of the Bible either. Most people in Scripture did not receive miraculous callings. God can guide our steps in many ways, and a miracle of this sort is just one way. I'm sure it's okay to desire such an experience, but we probably shouldn't stop moving forward with our lives in order to wait for one. God has already told us what he's looking for—it is embodied in Jesus and written in the Bible. If he has additional tasks for us, we can seek and discern those with God's help. He will make it clear.

It's also important to note that vocations are usually *formed* over time rather than discovered in an instant. While Scripture records instances of direct, even verbal (literal), callings, there are many more who received their responsibilities in other ways, and this seems to be the common experience for most of us today. Our responsibilities emerge over time through circumstances, opportunities, and wisdom from our communities.

CHALLENGES TO VOCATION DISCERNMENT

So how should we actually go about discerning our vocations? What are the nuts and bolts? These questions are clearly important and practical, and not just in a general way. We each want to know, personally, how to live our lives and what to invest ourselves in.

The communities we inhabit seek to answer this question for us, don't they? The images we consume on social media carry implicit and appealing messages about who we should be and what we should do. Scrolling through my feed, I've felt the tug of someone else's version of "the good life." Social media isn't the only place where this happens. Our own families and cultures of origin often impress on us something I call *vocational hierarchies*. A vocational hierarchy is an implicit ranking of callings embedded in a given culture. As I've reflected over the last few years about vocational development, I've discovered all sorts of vocation hierarchies. Here are a few of them:

- Nonprofit careers are more virtuous than for-profit careers because we can help people.

- For-profit careers are more virtuous than nonprofit or missions work because they grow economies and lead to prosperity for others.

- Crosscultural mission work is best because God calls us to evangelism and sacrifice.

- Being a homemaker is a more appropriate and personally fulfilling goal for female students than is paid work.

- Being a homemaker requires less skill and effort compared to paid employment.

- Being a doctor or attorney is a higher calling than other jobs because few people are intellectually gifted enough to practice these professions.

- Blue collar work is inferior to white collar work because it doesn't require as much intelligence or years of schooling.

Let's just pause for a moment to recognize that God doesn't put stock in such hierarchies. These are human inventions. It's also important to note that if you are a member of an ethnic minority, a woman, a first-generation college student, or are otherwise marginalized or experience disadvantage in some way, you will probably face barriers that others won't. It could be that the social and economic mobility that is in abundance around you is harder for you to get your hands on. You may have to work twice as hard just to gain a seat at the table, to get the interview, to be considered for promotion, or to be heard in the meeting. And what's more, your supervisors and co-workers may be ignorant of the unique challenges you face and the unique value you can offer. W. E. B. DuBois wrote about *double consciousness* more than a hundred years ago, and it still applies today. Double consciousness is the requirement that black people (and there are similar dynamics that govern the experiences of other minority groups as well) have to learn how to operate in two societies just in order to get ahead.[2]

In addition to the unconscious messages we encounter from our communities, there is another factor that makes vocational discernment difficult for us: at full bloom, consumerism becomes a chief framework through which we often approach vocational discernment. We shop for our college, our major, our leadership roles, and our jobs, which smuggles in the risk of turning people, experiences, and callings into commodities.

When we inadvertently approach our vocations in the same way that we approach our purchases, we quickly face something psychologists call *choice paralysis*. The basic idea is that when faced with more and more options, we have a harder time making a choice. My early, feeble attempts at grocery shopping are a great example. On one such trip when I was in college, I remember standing in front of a wall of ketchups, unable to make a decision. It makes sense—the more options there are, the harder we have to think about it. And over time we will inevitably accumulate decisions that we regret, which makes future choices feel riskier. Psychologists call the cumulative avoidance of decision-making *anticipated regret*.[3] This combination of proliferating options with anticipated regret can make us averse to making decisions, and not just about what ketchup to purchase but also the weightier considerations around our vocations. Please remember as you approach your future prospects that all vocational decisions are imperfect. None of them will satisfy you on their own.

When we have a significant decision to make, we should consider the options, reflect on relevant information, seek guidance, and then make our decision. That's generally the healthy way, but it can be anxious work wondering how our lives will turn out. As students experience this anxiety, I see them react in a few unhealthy ways. Some of them never start the hard work of discernment in the first place. They seem to avoid hard questions altogether as if there is no need to grow, no need to change anything. Life is good right now, so why change it? Others recognize the need to develop, but they skip the hard work of discernment and instead take someone else's ready-made plan for their lives. Some of our parents and our peers are all too ready to supply such a plan for us. Those who are tempted to accept someone else's plan for their lives may find it easier that way, but they're at risk of not really growing up, not really becoming an adult.

Other students jump into the disorienting work of exploration and discovery, but then they never arrive. They are scared of committing to a course of action, so they remain in the ether of exploration and indecision for too long. These are all easy traps to fall into.

And here's the kicker. Christians sometimes use the language of calling to baptize our dysfunctional courses of action. Perhaps the most common example is someone who gives more of their attention, time, and emotional energy to one role and robs their other roles of emotional investment. Sometimes the language of calling is used to make a pastor's workaholism look commendable, but their family suffers the consequences. And students aren't off the hook either: students who are "called" to a, b, or c may actually be avoiding x, y, or z. These traps offer a way out of the things that make us anxious about the future, but in the end they all rob us of important dimensions of our paths through life: recognizing the need to grow, doing the difficult work of discernment, and saying yes to some things and no to other things.

ASKING MORE AND BETTER QUESTIONS

When we ask vocational questions, we are usually wondering about new things that we might decide to do. We confront the question of what major we should pursue. We consider which profession or job track to approach. *What college should I attend? What major should I take? What class should I enroll in? What jobs should I apply for?* These are questions about the future directions of our lives, the roles we may or may not opt for. They are *what* questions.

Of course, *what* questions are important vocational questions. Admittedly, we do ask other questions too, like whether and whom we might want to marry or where we might live, but for the most part, we seem to ask a lot of what questions. But there is a whole deep and rich world of vocational considerations that these questions cannot begin to open. That's why I want you to start adding some new questions to your vocational discernment process—a few new friends to accompany you on life's journey. For some of you, vocational discernment is mostly an economic question—what should I do to maximize my earning potential? For others, it is about maximizing something else. Whatever that thing is for you, my hope is to expand the number of factors that you take into account in your decision making. In addition to *what*, I want to you add *who*, *when*, *where*, *why*, and *how* questions.

Who questions:

- Who will I share community with?
- Who are my neighbors?
- Whose advice am I listening to?
- Who am I? Who am I becoming?
- Whose friendship will I pursue?
- Whose opinions matter to me?
- Whose life scripts have I accepted as authoritative in my life and why?

When questions:

- At what life stage am I in right now and what does that mean for me and those around me?
- When should I expect to reach certain goals or benchmarks? Why have I set this particular pace? If I feel urgency, is it legitimate?
- When do I expect things to happen in my life?

Where questions:

- Where are the communities I am already a member of?
- Where will I build a home and put down roots?
- What does home mean to me? How and where will I create one?
- What scripts about locations and places have captured my imagination? Should I reexamine these scripts?

Why questions:

- Why do I make some decisions and not others? Am I really seeking personal security? Prestige? Or am I seeking to base my decisions on more holistic values?
- Why do I spend my time the way I do? How do I relate to the narrative that life is about a series of successes that include things

like marriage, owning a home, sending my kids to college, and
so on?

How questions:

- How do I approach my current vocations? What basic attitudes
  do I bring to my responsibilities?

- How will I engage in my roles with my communities—with my
  family, at school, at work, and so on?

In addition to expanding your repertoire of vocational questions, I
also want you to recalibrate the time frame in which you ask your questions. For some reason, we often assume that vocational discernment
relates to the realm of the future. We ask questions about what to do
in the future. But before vocation occurs *then*, it is occurring *now.*

We all have vocations right now, and I would argue that practicing
our present vocations is actually more important than deciding on our
future vocations. At the very least we should recognize how connected
our ability to discern and commit ourselves to our present responsibilities and roles is to our success in any future roles we might play. So,
I suggest that you pull the horizon of your vocational reflections right
out of the future and into the present. Thus, *what should I do in the
future* becomes *what should I do right now?* And *what communities would
I like to join in the future* becomes *what communities am I already part of?*
And *what kind of person would I like to become in the future* becomes *what
is the best version of myself right now?* Indeed, many, if not most, of our
vocations are not chosen—they are already given to us: our family, our
neighborhood, our communities.

BEYOND VOCATIONAL QUESTIONS
TO VOCATIONAL DISCIPLINES

In the years that I've been studying vocational discernment, it has
become clear that we think vocational discernment requires a technique. We think you're supposed to use a battery of diagnostic questions so you can figure out what to do with your life. That's why so
much of recent Christian literature on vocation is built around the

same old questions: What are your gifts? What are your passions? What needs and opportunities are out there? This approach is widespread. The questions themselves aren't the problem, per se—it's the fact that we almost approach our vocations like we're shopping. We want an efficient process for selecting the vocations that will make us happiest, which reminds me of how I approach my online shopping cart.

What if vocational discernment doesn't need a technique as much as patience and openness? What if it's as much about the process as it is about the destination? What if it's more about the communion we can have with God and others and less about the achievements we may accrue along the way? I'm tipping my cards, of course. I think that vocational life is less about achievement, independence, and success and more about submission, communion, and interdependence. It's more about giving and receiving than it is about earning and spending.

I'm arguing that the work of vocational discernment starts years before we ever pick up a book on the subject. It starts before we ever think to ask the recommended "vocational discernment questions" or take a personal assessment. This deeper work of vocational discernment starts in early childhood, in the values and priorities, the assumptions and convictions that grow in us over time. Vocational discernment is first about who we are becoming. It's a matter of spiritual formation before it is ever a technique. To put it in terms we talked about earlier, it is about our *general* calling before it's about our *particular* callings.

Because vocational discernment is first about your spiritual formation, I suggest that in addition to the *who, what, when, where, why,* and *how* questions we discussed earlier, you consider the role of spiritual disciplines in your vocational discipleship. All of the vocational discernment questions in the world won't produce the desired result unless you're also attending to more fundamental matters of the heart.[4] Kyle Bennett picks up on an important point in his *Practices of Love:* we think of spiritual disciplines as helping us grow closer to God, and we often miss the fact that they can also help us grow closer to others. The disciplines are there to help us better embody the greatest commandments, to love God *and our neighbors*. He calls it "flipping the disciplines on their side."[5]

Bennett goes on to contrast the "contemporary Christian view" of spiritual disciplines with what he calls "the horizontal view."[6] The contemporary view tends to treat spiritual disciplines as if they exist for our personal benefit, whereas the horizontal (which he is arguing for) emphasizes that spiritual disciplines exist for our *neighbor's benefit*. In this view, if you neglect to practice the disciplines you are robbing your neighbor of blessings. The contemporary view also tends to treat the disciplines as if they are distinct and separate from the daily tasks of life, but in the horizontal view disciplines meld with the existing rhythms and routines of your life. The contemporary view tends to treat disciplines as personal and private, and the horizontal view treats them as individual but also as corporate and communal.

So, what does a horizontal approach to the disciplines look like in practical terms? The author writes about fasting and feasting, meditation, solitude, silence, and a variety of other disciplines, but he always comes at them from the side. For example, practicing silence helps us renew how we speak with other people, and practicing solitude helps us renew how we socialize with others. These practices help us learn how to engage in these mundane activities as an expression of neighborly love. In other words, these practices help us approach the normal, everyday activities of our lives, one might say the *vocational* activities of our lives, *as spiritual disciplines*. It's really an outstanding insight.

If you are already practicing the spiritual disciplines "flipped on their side," when it's time to ask vocational discernment questions, you'll have deep resources to draw on because your values will be clearer, your priorities will be a little straighter, and your heart and mind will be ready for you to take a step. I'm not saying that vocational discernment will be easy (for some of you, it will be easy; for some, very difficult), but only that you will have deeper resources from which to draw as you consider your vocational paths forward. As you practice these disciplines "flipped on their side" I want you to keep three vocational discernment tasks in mind:

1. Take on the mind of Christ.

2. Grow in your acceptance of yourself.

3. Tend to your roots.

Take on the mind of Christ. Did you know that you have a *vocational imagination*? It manifests in the many vocational images, aspirations, and dreams that inhabit your mental landscape. When you picture your future, what images come to mind? When you think about what job you might do, whether you are married, have children, where you will live, and what life will be like, what desires do you feel tugging at your heart?

Your vocational imagination requires tending, much like a garden. Merely going to church and checking the Christian boxes aren't sufficient on their own, and without thinking about this purposefully, your imagination will grow the weeds haphazardly cast into your mind by the vocational hierarchies and social media feeds we have already discussed. Your vocational imagination will look a little like the garden in my back yard, disordered and overgrown. In *The Confessions*, Augustine wrote profoundly about how our loves are disordered, that we love some things more than we should and other things less than we should. And here's the thing about your vocational imagination: it can lead you to love some things more and other things less. So, the key question is, does your imagination help you to love God and others more and to love lesser things less? You might want to spend a little time reflecting on what it means to take on the mind of Christ as it is described in Philippians 2:1-11. As you'll see, the most enriching ingredient you can work into the soil of your vocational imagination is Christlikeness. You can almost watch as the mind of Christ growing in you judges, renews, and reconfigures the content of your vocational imagination.

Grow in your acceptance of yourself. We all wrestle with two vocational selves, a *real self* and an *ideal self*, and with the wide gap that we sense between them. The problem is that we are willing to sacrifice far too much in order to attain the ideal we cherish. Do you know any people who are sick with workaholism? They might be neglecting other responsibilities and relationships as they give more and more energy and attention to a single job. They may be striving to resolve the gap they feel between who they know they are and the ideal self that drives them. They have become slaves to an illusion.

We should strive to clear away the idealism and cynicism that cloud our self-understanding, that we should seek to know and accept who we are fundamentally, even as we seek to grow and become the best versions of ourselves. This clearheaded understanding of yourself means a few things. First, it means that you accept that you are a creature, flawed, limited, and imperfect, but also that you are made in God's image. You are a walking glory or, as C. S. Lewis has put it, an "everlasting splendour."[7] With this basic understanding of yourself in mind, you can move forward without an expectation of vocational perfection, without holding yourself to impossible standards. The second step is taking stock of your spiritual gifts, your talents, your values, as well as your weaknesses and challenges. This can be scary work because it means confronting and looking squarely at your imperfect self (and this is getting more and more difficult in this picture-perfect, social media-saturated age). This task can also be intimidating, especially if there are people in your life who have strong opinions about what you should do and who you should be. But this is exactly the moment when you should set aside any voices that seem to demand your allegiance and listen carefully to the voice of God and to the signals in your life.

Illusions, myths, idealisms and other departures from reality seem to plague not only our self-understanding but also honesty about our circumstances. It's certainly possible to see vocational opportunities where there aren't any, but perhaps more importantly, we may also fail to see opportunities where they do exist. It's not that dreams are unhelpful or should be avoided, but it is a sweet gift to be released from the pressure of living up to an ideal.

Tend to your roots. In this age of increased globalization, urbanization, and mobility, our vocational imagination is often bent toward the things that are "out there" not "right here." But distant and future vocations aren't real yet, not real like your present and proximate vocations toward your family, your friends, your roommate, your summer job, and your role as a student. You have a present responsibility toward the vocations you already have, vocations that are rooted to the communities you inhabit now, and perhaps where you've lived in the past. Your taproot is located somewhere. Where? And how will you serve that community?

The thing about roots is that they spread out over the course of the life of a tree. You are not bound to one or the other. Your roots can anchor to multiple communities: to your church, neighborhood, family, friends, to your community in the city where you used to live, and now to the communities around your home in a new city. But remember that roots that don't find nutrition sources can atrophy and must grow toward new resources to survive and thrive.

CONCLUSION

The Gospel of Matthew reports:

> When the ten heard it, they were angry with the two brothers. But Jesus called them to him and said, "You know that the rulers of the Gentiles lord it over them, and their great ones are tyrants over them. It will not be so among you; but whoever wishes to be great among you must be your servant, and whoever wishes to be first among you must be your slave; just as the Son of Man came not to be served but to serve, and to give his life a ransom for many." (Mt 20:24-28 NRSV)

In his book *The Road to Character*, David Brooks seems to have had something like Matthew 20 in mind when he wrote about the differences between our "résumé virtues" and our "eulogy virtues." Résumé virtues are the habits that help us achieve social status, expand our earning potential, climb the ladder, get famous, and so on. These habits help us "crush it" out there. Eulogy virtues, on the other hand, are habits that help us be good friends to each other, to invest deeply in our relationships and communities, to serve those in need, and to make our own contributions to the common good, all the things we hope people will say about us at our funerals. His point isn't to say that résumé virtues like ambition, diligence, and competition are wrong in and of themselves, but rather that we should subject them to the supervision of more important virtues. Jesus seems to do just that as he reminds James and John that their "résumé virtues" needed to be flipped upside down, that "whoever wishes to be great among you must be your servant."

So, as you make vocational decisions about where to go to college, what major to choose, and what jobs to pursue, seek first and foremost to embody Jesus' call to servanthood. The point I'm making here isn't so much about what you will do as about how and why you will do it. With the mind of Christ in view, your vocational discernment process will become a little less about pursuing personal success and a little more about communion and servanthood. Sometimes I actually wonder if the vocabulary of vocation gets in the way. Perhaps it is better simply to ask "what am I responsible for?" and Jesus made that mercifully clear: love God and love your neighbor. Once we've made this our starting point, the role of discernment becomes a way of working out in the particulars of our lives the unique ways we will fulfill this greatest of all vocations.

Chapter Three

Gender Roles

EMILY HUNTER McGOWIN

I WAS TWO MONTHS INTO MY FIRST SEMESTER as a PhD student in theology when my husband, Ronnie, and I discovered that we were expecting our second child. Our first child was only seven months old—not even crawling yet. This was, shall we say, less than ideal. I responded with a variety of emotions, managing to feel excited, disappointed, joyful, anxious, amazed, and afraid, all at the same time. "The plan" had been to have one child before entering the PhD program, complete the program, find a job, and then—and only then!—have more children. But that plan was out the window. What now?

I had plenty of reasons to worry. I was afraid for my sanity and stamina. Doctoral programs are a lot of work—stressful for minds and bodies in their own right. I was afraid for the resilience of our marriage. It was difficult enough with one child while doing a PhD, but now we were adding another. I was also carrying a hefty load of mommy guilt from years of being told (subtly and not-so-subtly) that mothers who pursue careers are selfish and doomed to failure. And I wasn't sure how my pregnancy would be greeted by my department. What would my professors and colleagues think? Did we have maternity leave? (We didn't. More about that later.) Eventually, though, one issue emerged as the most concerning: Can I keep going? Should I keep going? Can I be a mom and a theologian at the same time?

Despite my inner turmoil, I was married to a man with deep confidence in my calling. When I was uncertain and wavering, he was resolutely committed to doing what was necessary to see my vocation lived out. He had been this way from the beginning. On our first date, Ronnie had listened patiently as I listed all of my concerns about pursuing a career in theology while also wanting to be a wife and mother. And when I finally stopped, he smiled and said, "Emily, I don't think you should have to choose between your calling and your family. You can do both. We can do both." He was as good as his word.

After the shock of our unplanned pregnancy wore off, Ronnie helped me find the courage and endurance to continue on our chosen path. He even put his career on hold in order to be the full-time caregiver to our two—eventually three—young children while I finished my PhD. Today, Ronnie is a pastor and I am a theologian, and together we have been navigating the challenges of being a dual-vocation couple for almost sixteen years.

As I reflect on this event almost a decade later, I think the primary problem I faced was one of imagination. I needed a vision of what life could look like as a woman with a marriage, children, and career. Having never seen it done, I was at a loss. I wondered, *How is this supposed to work?* And I'm not the only one. Many Christian women, especially those raised in American evangelicalism, grow up with few examples of what it looks like for a woman to pursue a career and raise children at the same time. In fact, some of us find ourselves in environments where it is communicated quite strongly that women with careers and a family are self-centered and greedy. We need a new way of thinking about work and womanhood.

But women aren't the only ones asking these kinds of questions. Young men have similar concerns, especially as they are coming of age in a society where the ideal of *the* man as sole breadwinner doesn't always pan out. Are so-called traditional gender roles the only options for married life? What if I can't find suitable employment, and my wife has to be the primary wage-earner? Is it okay for me to take a less prestigious position so my wife can pursue her dream job? Am I still a "real man" if I choose to be a stay-at-home dad?

The way one answers these questions about gender and vocation will necessarily depend on the way one interprets Scripture, theology, culture, and history. Not everyone will give the same answer. But there is no biblical blueprint for discerning one's work as a Christian woman or man in the contemporary world. Certainly, we know some of what we are meant to be and do as Christians. We are to abide in Christ and bear much fruit (Jn 15:4, 8). We are to walk by the Spirit and present our everyday, ordinary lives as a living sacrifice to God (Gal 5:25; Rom 12:1). We are to love one another as Christ has loved us (Jn 13:34). And these clear scriptural admonitions go a long way toward guiding our behavior on any given day. But the particulars of our vocations are another matter. The Bible doesn't say what job you should take after college or whether you should take time off to be a stay-at-home mom.

If there are no blueprints, then we are in the position of having to discern bit-by-bit, step-by-step what faithfulness looks like within our specific context. We have to make it up as we go along. We have to improvise. This is, in fact, what Ronnie and I have been doing for our entire marriage. Inspired by theologian Frederick Bauerschmidt, I like to call it Spirit-led improvisation.[1] By the leading of the Holy Spirit, with the guidance of Scripture, in communion with the church, by the example of the saints, and through the details of our particular life circumstances, we have to improvise the course of our lives. And if your future involves marriage, you will have a lifelong partner (and maybe children) with whom to improvise too.

But before we can improvise well, we have to know the story we find ourselves in—the biblical story, that is. And as it turns out, from the very beginning Scripture has a lot to say about women, men, and work.

WOMEN AND MEN AS COWORKERS

According to the first chapters of the biblical narrative, work plays a central role in what it means to be human. According to Genesis 1:28, after the creation of human beings in God's image, God commands them, male and female, to increase in number, fill the earth, subdue it, and rule over the rest of God's creatures. In Genesis 2, Adam is placed in the Garden of Eden to "work it and take care of it" (Gen 2:15). Thus, the Creator God delegates to humanity the responsibility of caring for and cultivating God's creation.

In this endeavor, Adam and Eve are partners. In Genesis 2, God makes Eve to be a "suitable helper" or "helper corresponding to" (Heb. *ezer kenegdo*) to Adam. There's no sense of subordination here. The most common usage of *ezer* in the Old Testament is to refer to God's activity as a "helper" to Israel (see, for example, Ex 18:4; Deut 33:29; Ps 33:20). Rather, Eve is Adam's complementary coworker in the cultivation of the world.[2]

Unfortunately, this harmonious partnership doesn't last long. The story in Genesis 3 is well-known: The serpent lies, fruit is taken, given, and eaten, and then the first couple's eyes are opened. The disobedience of Adam and Eve is followed by shame, confrontation, and blame-shifting. Their transgression of God's commands leads to terrible consequences. Now, childbearing comes only through pain; work comes only through drudgery and toil; and the former easy partnership between Adam and Eve is poisoned at the root: "Your desire will be for your husband, and he will rule over you" (Gen 3:16).

Because of the fall, men and women no longer relate to each other as they should. Sinful patterns of domination, exploitation, and subordination have characterized men and women's relationships for centuries. What it means to be human, what it means to be male and female, and what it means to work have all been clouded and marred by the effects of sin.

Still, a message of hope is hidden in the same chapter where the fall is described. In Genesis 3:15, the Lord says to the serpent,

> And I will put enmity
> > between you and the woman,
> > and between your offspring and hers;
> he will crush your head,
> > and you will strike his heel.

This verse has come to be called the *protoevangelium* because many Christian theologians see in it the first trace of God's intention to send a deliverer through the descendants of Adam and Eve, who will, by his death, crush the serpent once and for all and free humanity from sin and death. Indeed, it is the power of Jesus Christ's death and resurrection that allows us, male and female, to be loosed from the curse of domination and subordination outlined in Genesis 3:16. Through Christ, we can be restored to full partnership in God's created order, living out our respective vocations side by side once again.

WOMEN'S WORK AND MEN'S WORK

The story of the Bible reveals that all human beings, men and women, have a vocation in God's creation. The kind of work we do, the context of our work, the remuneration for our work, and the negotiation of our work in relation to other responsibilities—all of these things must be navigated by the guidance of the Spirit. But the fact that all human beings—male and female, single and married, mothers and fathers—are intended by God to be workers, cultivators, inventors, shapers, and co-creators in God's world is beyond dispute.

Still, there remains a lot of ongoing confusion about the nature of "women's work" and "men's work." I think this confusion can be traced to Adam and Eve's original betrayal. What women and men fundamentally are, in the essence of their being, remains a mystery to us, both because we are finite creatures and because sin has affected our ability to interpret God's world. Left to our own devices, we come up with models of femininity and masculinity that are deeply flawed. Certainly, gender is linked to the human body and the biological sex that body is born with. But much of what passes for femininity and masculinity today is, as many now realize, culturally constructed. What we consider "girly" or "boyish" has as much to do with our cultural moment as it does any universal truths about what it means to be male or female.

The Bible also testifies to this complexity. In a narrative landscape that includes a rich diversity of both male and female figures, who is to say what attributes are really and truly masculine or feminine?

Moreover, Scripture does not provide a universal definition of masculine or feminine. Due to the diversity of male and female persons and the lack of clear-cut definitions, attempts to pin down what is truly "biblical manhood" and "biblical womanhood" are doomed to failure. Such efforts almost always result in culturally bound stereotypes—what I call *gender blueprints*—that exclude just as many as they include. The truth is, there are as many ways to be womanly as there are women, and as many ways to be manly as there are men.

Jesus Christ, the Son of God incarnate, is the fullest revelation of what it means to be human, male or female. That is to say, the meaning of our humanity, whatever our gender, is revealed to us in the person and life of Jesus Christ. Yes, Jesus of Nazareth was a man, but he does not save us by his maleness. Rather, he saves us by his humanness. That is why he is the Savior of both men and women. Both male and female Christians are called to be imitators of Christ in the particularities of their sexed and gendered bodies. Much more important than the fulfillment of gender stereotypes, therefore, is the pursuit of Christlikeness. And as we walk by the Spirit, he dispenses gifts to the members of Christ's body, not on the basis of sex or gender, but out of sheer gratuitous love "so that the body of Christ may be built up" (Eph 4:12).

Now, some Christians insist that the Bible does, in fact, provide gender blueprints for men and women. They argue from the Bible that, generally speaking, men are ordained by God to lead—in home, church, and the world—and women are ordained by God to support and follow. Though the particulars can vary, this general perspective among Protestants is called complementarianism.[3] And they sometimes teach that women should not serve in jobs where they will be exercising authority over men or doing things that will violate divinely ordained gender roles. For example, someone with a complementarian perspective might not have a problem with a woman working as a lower-level associate in a corporation, but they might object to a woman becoming vice president because in that position she will be the direct superior for male employees. Exercising such significant authority over men, they say, goes against the grain of God's design for men and women.

I respect my complementarian sisters and brothers, but I don't hold to such rigid notions of gender roles. Many volumes have been devoted to this subject, so I won't attempt to review their arguments here. But I want to be clear that I don't reject complementarian notions of gender *despite* the Bible; I reject such notions *because* of the Bible. In my view, Scripture does not define narrowly what men and women are, nor restrict women's work to the private sphere of hearth and home, nor demarcate women's work and men's work based on gender.

If you survey the entire biblical story from Genesis to Revelation, you find women doing many things that defy so-called traditional roles for women. (Can they be traditional roles if so many prominent women in the Bible actually defied them?) In the Old Testament, Miriam is a leader of Israel alongside her brothers, Moses and Aaron. She directs the people of God in worship and her words are recorded in Scripture. Deborah is a judge, serving as prophet, political leader, judicial decision-maker, and deliverer for God's people. She leads the armies of Israel into battle and her words are recorded in Scripture as well. Huldah is a prophet during the reign of Josiah who was called on to confirm the veracity of the Torah and speak the words of God to the king. Even the often-cited "Proverbs 31 woman" is not a paragon of quiet domesticity but an archetype of wise, righteous, and industrious living in both private and public spheres. The wise woman is an example for all to follow, male or female.

In the New Testament, Mary Magdalene is the first witness to the resurrection and the one Jesus sends to proclaim the good news for the first time. If an apostle is "one sent with a message," then Mary Magdalene was the apostle to the apostles. Junia is called "foremost among the apostles" and serves with Andronicus (likely her husband) as a traveling missionary, which would have involved evangelizing, teaching, and leading churches (Rom 16:7). Priscilla, along with her husband, Aquila, is a friend of the apostle Paul and a teacher of the Bible and theology who "explained . . . the way of God more accurately" to Apollos (Acts 18:26). Phoebe is a deacon and benefactor of the early church, sent by Paul to deliver his letter to the Romans and to explain its contents to the people (Rom 16:1-2).

More could be said, obviously. But the point is, women are very influential in the story of God's people, and most of them do not conform to complementarian gender roles. Women are leaders, prophets, teachers, and decision-makers. Women serve as examples of righteousness, courage, and wisdom. Indeed, the women of Scripture are proof that vocations are not determined based on sex and gender, but on the call of God and power of the Holy Spirit—in addition to things like skills, abilities, and circumstances.

There are a handful of passages from the letters of Paul that complementarians (and others) believe limit the work of women in the world (1 Cor 11:2-16; 14:34-35; Eph 5:22-24; 1 Tim 2:11-15; Titus 2:3-5). But this is by no means the only way to read such texts. Moreover, these passages have to be read in light of Paul's own practice of supporting women in public ministry. When considered in light of the whole sweep of Scripture and Paul's own practice, I agree with scholars like Scot McKnight who conclude that the limitations Paul appears to place on women in some of his letters are heavily context dependent. That is to say, Paul's limitations are aimed at the specific circumstances of the churches to which he's writing and the social and cultural context of the first century. As such, they do not translate into universal prohibitions on public work for women today.[4]

In conclusion, therefore, there is nothing within the Bible that suggests women or men are disqualified from certain kinds of work simply because of their gender. We have a long way to go before society is rid of stereotypes for what constitutes "women's work" and "men's work," but the Christian community can lead the way in dismantling these stereotypes. In fact, if we are truly a new creation in Christ, then it is part of our mission to model a new way to be human to the watching world. A man's work is manly when a man is doing it. A woman's work is womanly when a woman is doing it. So, the question is not whether your gender allows you to pursue certain vocational paths. The question, instead, is this: Do you have the proper gifts, training, temperament, and personality for the work you feel called to?

SOME HISTORICAL AND CULTURAL PERSPECTIVE

Of course, even with the guidance of Scripture, we don't discern matters of vocation in a vacuum. How can we be sure we aren't confusing cultural norms for biblical duties? Understanding how history and culture have influenced our ways of thinking about gender and work is vital for our discernment.

The truth is, women have always worked. Women in the Bible most certainly worked. But women throughout history have worked too. Agrarian societies have been the norm for most of human history. Within these settings, women and men worked very hard, both inside and outside the home. Katelyn Beaty sums it up well: "All except the most elite women of society . . . have had no choice but to work by the sweat of their brows. For most of human history, work was life and life was work. And men and women labored interdependently in order to provide the daily bread for kin and community."[5] Among other things, this means the evangelical ideal of the stay-at-home mom—a woman solely devoted to raising children and managing the private household— is a thoroughly modern phenomenon. How, then, did we get here?

Between the late 1700s and mid-1800s, the Western world underwent seismic shifts as a result of the Industrial Revolution and the dawn of modern capitalism. And these shifts also spread beyond the Western world. Farms were replaced by factories. Craftsmen were replaced by machines. Home-based labor was replaced by city-based labor. The social and cultural consequences of these changes were enormous, especially in regard to notions of gender roles and public and private spheres. Men started leaving home to go to work, so wives and husbands often spent much of their days apart. And, as a result, public life and private life became firmly divided. Men made most of the decisions in the public realm of business, politics, and law, while women made most of the decisions in the private realm of home and family.

Also the public sphere of business and politics, where the "self-made man" pursued success and independence, was viewed as too harsh and sleazy for virtuous women. Instead, middle class white women were "assigned to domesticity inside the home and voluntary religious or charity work outside of it."[6] Meanwhile, black women, Native women, immigrant women, and poor women continued to have to work for wages outside the home—and do so to this day. But it was a mark of the middle-class white man's success that he could support his family on a single wage and afford the extravagance of a "housewife."

Thus, the evangelical Christian ideal of the virtuous housewife has its roots in the white, middle-class culture of the Victorian period. It seems odd, therefore, that so many Christians still cling to such notions of gender. Not only does the Bible not support the housewife ideal but there are many settings today in which women simply must work: single women, widowed women, women with disabled husbands, women whose husbands mismanage their finances, and women whose families need additional wages to survive. Given the historical and cultural roots of our gender stereotypes and the way they exclude a significant portion of the world's women, it's past time to reformulate how we imagine women, men, and work.

HAVING IT ALL?

Even as society as a whole is moving away from rigid notions of gender roles, debates persist about what women can expect to achieve. In American periodicals these debates often revolve around the question "Can women have it all?"[7] Of course, having it all is tricky to define. Most mean success and satisfaction in career, love, and family—all at the same time.

Before anything else, though, I think it's important to recognize what this kind of question implies. The perceived dilemma women face when it comes to their work and their personal lives is, generally speaking, not one faced by men. It is rare for people to wonder whether men can have it all. Few people wonder whether a devoted husband can also be a productive employee. Few people wonder whether a man with career ambitions can also be a loving father. But these questions are asked of women on a regular basis. That reality, in itself, indicates a problem in the way we think about women, men, and work.

Going further, Christians have a duty to question the very idea of having it all. The goal of the Christian life for women and men doesn't necessarily coincide with worldly conceptions of success. Faithfulness to Christ and his kingdom may not always lead to popular symbols of prosperity: marriage, home ownership, new cars, and lucrative investments. We simply cannot take for granted that this version of having it all is God's best for us—or best for our families, churches, and communities.

To make sure I'm really clear, let me say it another way: You don't have to get married to lead a faithful and fulfilling Christian life. You don't have to have children. You don't have to climb the corporate ladder. You don't have to own a large house or travel the world or write a bestseller or acquire fame and fortune. In fact, for most Christians throughout history, the faithful and fulfilling Christian life looked more like failure by worldly standards. And many of the Christians we hold up as exemplars—Dietrich Bonhoeffer, Dorothy Day, Mother Teresa, and Martin Luther King Jr., for example—are those for whom such status symbols were nowhere to be found.

With all of these caveats in mind, then, let's return to the controversial question, Can women have it all? Hidden in this inquiry, I think, is the same fundamental concern I had when faced with an unplanned pregnancy two months into my doctoral studies. Can women have a career while also being a wife and mother? I have learned that the answer to this question is complicated and involves several factors.

First, if marriage is in one's future, then it's important to see that marriage requires building a household while yoked in partnership with another. So, it is very important to marry someone committed to being a true partner in all areas of life: home, work, children, church, and more. Even the smoothest marriage requires practice at communication and compromise. It's not always straightforward who should do what and when, especially if you don't hold to prescribed gender roles. Studies show that married women end up doing significantly more housework than their spouses, even when both are employed full-time.[8] This ought not to be the case. Since most couples who work cannot afford extra domestic help in the form of cooks and maids, women and men will have to share household duties.

I still remember the Saturday morning, very early in our marriage, when I was writing a paper for graduate school and Ronnie was sweeping and doing laundry. I could tell he was upset about something. When I asked him what was wrong, he sighed deeply and responded, "I just feel like I'm doing your job for you!" That's when I realized my sweet husband was under the impression that housework was *my* work—and he didn't like having to pick up the slack! The discussion that followed that comment was a turning point in our relationship. We discovered that when it comes to a two-vocation household, there is no "women's work" and "men's work." It's all "our work," and couples have to figure out how to get everything done in an equitable way.

Parenthood is also a calling that involves significant work. Women who have children experience significant changes and challenges as a result. Pregnant and nursing mothers are vulnerable in ways that others are not. The physical demands of pregnancy, infancy, and toddlerhood are real and necessarily affect the way women relate to the world—including their jobs. Women who adopt or foster children deal with physical challenges, too, on top of other trials biological mothers may never face. Regardless of how one becomes a mother, though, there's no doubt that mothering is work—real physical, emotional, mental, and spiritual work. And while I've focused on the challenges facing mothers, I want to be clear that fathering involves serious and difficult labor as well. They might not be giving birth and nursing, but 3 a.m. infant wake-ups and 7 p.m. toddler meltdowns are physically, mentally, and spiritually demanding for fathers too. The point, though, is this: parenting is real work and it involves both parents.

Christian parents are called to raise their children in the knowledge and love of God. To choose to undertake the work of parenting on top of one's vocation in the public sphere is challenging, to say the least. But the delicate interplay of work, marriage, and children is something

all Christians must consider as they seek discernment about their vocation. The point is, learning how to be faithful spouses, parents, and
workers is a human concern, not just a woman's concern.

Now, having it all isn't just about the private dynamics of individual
couples navigating marriage and parenthood. There are broader social,
economic, and political factors that come to bear on women's (and
men's) lives too. The United States is the world's only industrialized
nation that doesn't have a federal paid maternity leave policy. And this
has real consequences for real women. As Beaty notes, "Policy isn't just
politics. Policy is always personal."[9] Because of workplace policies un-
friendly to mothers, many women feel they are forced to choose between succeeding at work and being a good parent. So, slowly, over
time, they make decisions that stunt their progress and edge them out
of leadership. Until these policies change, couples have to keep these
things in mind as they plan their lives together.

During my time there, the university where I completed my PhD did
not have an official maternity leave policy for graduate students. I had
essentially two options: continue working with a newborn or take an
unpaid leave of absence. Thankfully, our daughter was born in the
summer. But I was forced to return to work only three weeks after
giving birth. Juggling the work of doctoral seminars, teaching under-
grads, and caring for a nursing infant—all while very sleep-deprived—
was the most difficult thing I've ever done. I couldn't even get a parking
pass for a lot closer to my building to make the commute less taxing.
Change is coming, but it is coming slowly.

In addition to anti-family policies, mothers who want a career also
have to contend with the exorbitant costs of childcare, which regularly
exceed the price of rent or mortgage. When Ronnie and I realized in
year two of the PhD program how much money all-day childcare was
going to cost for our toddler and infant, we made the decision to share
childcare responsibilities. Ronnie took a part-time ministry job that
only required him to work Sundays, Tuesdays, and Thursdays. I had
seminars and teaching on Mondays, Wednesdays, and Fridays. When
he worked, the children were with me. When I worked, the children

were with him. It was a demanding schedule, and neither of us felt like we had enough time. I was forced to adjust my stringent (read: perfectionist) expectations for class preparation, teaching, and grades. But we made it through a difficult season by working together—and significantly reduced our monthly expenses in the process.

Beyond such challenges, women also have to contend with sometimes hostile work environments. A Pew Research study from 2017 revealed that about four-in-ten women say they've experienced gender discrimination at work. This discrimination takes many forms: being treated like they aren't competent, receiving less support from superiors, being passed over for assignments, and being denied opportunities for leadership. Expectations for women and men differ considerably, too, and those expectations lead to bias in the way women and men are reviewed and promoted. For example, men are allowed to be ambitious and aggressive, but women who do the same are perceived as hostile and cold. It takes a lot of intentional work to overcome such stereotypes while also pursuing excellence at your job—and not all workplaces will allow a woman to do so. All of the above is in addition to the fact that female full-time workers still earn, on average, only 80 percent of what men make.[10]

I will admit that in the face of these challenges, it would be easy to become angry and cynical. Women and men both bear the image of God, and they are meant to cultivate God's world side by side. Women possess "half of humanity's gifts, passions, and experiences."[11] So, when women are kept from fulfilling their callings, the world suffers for it. If we are convinced that women's work is essential to human flourishing, then we should be working together for communal solutions to the problems women face as they pursue their callings beyond the home.

STAY-AT-HOME MOMS . . . AND DADS!

But what about those who feel called to stay home with their children? Just as there is nothing in Scripture that suggests women should not work outside the home, so also there's nothing in Scripture that suggests women must work outside the home. Managing a household and raising children is real work, work that is simultaneously challenging and rewarding. Many women find a home-focused way of life to be satisfying in ways that a career is not. Fewer and fewer families in the United States are able to afford the financial arrangement of a single breadwinner, but those who can and want to focus their efforts on hearth and home are certainly free to do that.

Some women wonder if this would be a waste of their education and potential. But stay-at-home motherhood is only a waste of one's education and potential if you think managing a home and raising children does not require intelligence, character, and skill. In fact, being a stay-at-home mom (or dad!) requires all of the above. So, it is a perfectly valid choice to focus one's efforts on the rearing and educating of children over paid work outside the home.

The same holds true for stay-at-home dads. Even though American culture is still adjusting to this increasingly more common phenomenon, there's nothing unmanly about managing the home and serving as the primary caregiver for children. (Indeed, it's a strange gender ideology that says men are qualified to be leaders in the public sphere but not fit to raise their children and manage the domestic space.) There are many circumstances in which it would make sense for the husband to stay home with the children: if the wife can make more money, if daily childcare is too cost-prohibitive, if the child has special needs that dad is best equipped to meet, or if the family's quality of life is better with one spouse devoted to the children.

The point is, both women and men are free to choose to make raising children their primary work. These decisions must be discerned in the various contexts we find ourselves in, with the guidance of the Holy Spirit, by the wisdom of Scripture, in fellowship with the community of faith. My only caveat, though, is this: even if you give the majority of your time to your parental vocation, you should always have an eye toward the way you've been gifted and equipped to contribute to the world around you. All parents have a vocation to raise their children in the love of God. But they also have a vocation to contribute in some way to the remaking of creation under Christ's lordship.

So, stay-at-home parents should seek to find the place in their realm of influence where, in the words of Frederick Buechner, their deep gladness and the world's deep hunger meet.[12] Beyond your home and your children, what is the kind of work that you need most to do and the world needs most to be done? It could be organizing volunteers at the food pantry, tutoring students in algebra, assisting with voter registration drives, or teaching art classes at the public library. Find that thing and make time to do it. Everyone involved in the work of parenting has something to contribute to the world, too, even if it is not your full-time work and even if you don't get paid wages to do it.

SPIRIT-LED IMPROVISATION

Discovering that there is no gender-based blueprint for our lives can be both freeing and frightening. On the one hand, many are relieved to know they are not limited by cultural stereotypes about femininity and masculinity, women's work and men's work. We are, indeed, free to pursue our sense of calling under the leadership of the Holy Spirit. What an exhilarating reality! On the other hand, gender blueprints can be useful—even comforting—because the roles we're supposed to play are predetermined and therefore predictable. There's not a lot of day-by-day negotiation in the traditional model of gender roles. The fixed gender blueprint provides a modicum of stability in an increasingly unstable world.

I understand the desire for stability and predictability. I am deeply sympathetic to it. But I believe clinging to such culturally bound models is both unbiblical and unworkable for our contemporary world. The good news is that even without gender blueprints we can still discern what faithful Christian work looks like within our various contexts. Whether your future involves singleness, marriage, or parenthood, whether your primary work will be public or domestic, all of us—men and women—can engage in the work of Spirit-led improvisation. Filled with the Holy Spirit, guided by the Scriptures, supported by the church, and encouraged by the example of the saints, we can discern a life of faithfulness and fulfillment as God works through us to make all things new.

Chapter Four

Sex

BETH FELKER JONES

A STUDENT TOLD ME A STORY about a small group she was part of in high school. The group's leader gave each of the girls a beautiful teacup. Each one was different, each lovely. Delicate china, gorgeously painted. The leader was teaching about sexual purity. She told the girls that they were like those teacups. Fragile and beautiful. They needed to protect that fragile beauty, to lock those cups away in a china cabinet where they'd be safe from damage. To sin sexually would be to break that beautiful cup.

My student wanted to be pure, but she was also dating someone she found powerfully attractive, and she told me how she'd been having sex with her boyfriend for several months. She felt like a broken teacup. Cracked. Useless. Ruined and inappropriate for display.

She also felt like there was no point in changing her sexual behavior now that she had "lost" her sexual purity. She felt guilty and irredeemable. I think this student's youth leader meant well, and she was right about one thing: our bodies are precious to God.

But the precious teacup view of sexuality is fundamentally un-Christian, because it (1) is mostly for girls and not for boys, (2) ignores the whole great story of sin and redemption, including God's promises of healing and grace, and (3) denies that humans are precious sons and daughters of the King, who bear that King's royal image, and instead reduces humans to things. More, the lesson about the teacups made it very hard for my student to understand God's love and care for her, and it also made it hard for her to find hope in God's good plans for her as a sexual being, called to witness to God's goodness with all the choices she makes with her body.

Because I write and teach about sex, lots of students talk to me about what it means to be a Christian and to honor God with our sexuality. I talk to Christians who have never dated, who are longing for intimacy, and who feel "less than" because they don't have a boyfriend or girlfriend and fear they won't find a spouse. I talk to people who are dating and wonder about how to maintain healthy boundaries in those relationships, and people—like my student—who are crossing those boundaries and are awash in shame and guilt. I talk to people who have been assaulted and abused, and I talk to people who think sex is dirty and shameful and fear sexual intimacy. I talk to people who "know" Christians aren't supposed to have sex outside of marriage but who don't know how that could be possible, or why this is a teaching of Christian faith in the first place.

All of these precious people need a story to help them understand sex and sexuality. We need a story that makes sense with what we choose to do with our bodies. We need some gospel (literally "good news") about sex. Fortunately, Christian faith gives us a much better story than the precious teacup story. In the Christian story, human beings exist to tell the world about the love and glory of God. Human sexuality exists to be a witness to the world about the love and glory of God.

SEX AND THE CHRISTIAN STORY

From the beginning, Christians were strange about sexual ethics. We've always been weird. Different. Deeply at odds with the surrounding culture. And from the beginning, you couldn't understand Christian sexual ethics without understanding the bigger Christian story, because Christians have always believed that sex reflects something about who God is. Christian sexual ethics aren't about following a set of rules, and they aren't about protecting breakable teacups. They're about telling the story of God's faithfulness to God's people.

In the book of Hosea, God instructs the prophet Hosea to marry a prostitute named Gomer and to be radically faithful to her. The marriage between Hosea and Gomer is a metaphor for God's radical faithfulness to the people of Israel. Even though we humans are unfaithful, God "allures" and speaks "tenderly" to us (Hos 2:14). God is like our "husband" and promises "I will take you for my wife forever; I will take you for my wife in righteousness and in justice, in steadfast love, and in mercy. I will take you for my wife in faithfulness; and you shall know the LORD" (Hos 2:19-20 NRSV). When we—by the grace and power of God—are able to practice faithfulness in marriage and celibacy in singleness, we use our bodies to tell the story of God's radical faithfulness.

We all know why Christians are seen as strange about sex in our current world, but why were Christians strange in the early centuries of the church? It was because Christian sexual ethics wanted to tell this story—the story of radical devotion to a faithful God—a different story than the dominating story of the Roman Empire.

THE CHRISTIAN STORY IN THE ROMAN WORLD

Rome, like our world, had its own sexual ethics. For citizens, women were supposed to be chaste outside of marriage and faithful within marriage, so their husbands could be absolutely sure they were the fathers of their children. Women were also supposed to have babies for the good of the father and the state. Babies meant the family and the empire had a future.

Male citizens weren't subject to as many restraints as their sisters and wives. They were free to have sex with many partners, both male and female, but they were expected to show a certain amount of self-discipline as a sign of their manliness. They also were expected to be in control, so a man could have sex with another man, so long as he was the dominant partner.

For slaves, both male and female, forced sex was the norm. They could be used by their owners or were prostituted. Their bodies served the whims of the powerful men of Rome, allowing those men an outlet for their sexual "freedom" while "protecting" the chastity of the higher-class women of Rome.

Rome's sexual ethics tells a story. The heroes are the manly men of Rome, the fathers who control their families and the state. The happy ending is the perpetuation of the strength of the empire. The story has victims too; chief among them, the slaves whose bodies were abused by men with power.

Early Christianity astounded the Roman Empire when it challenged this story with a radically new sexual ethic attached to a radically different story. Christian heroes are not Roman men, strong in power and full of virility, but both men and women who claim to have no power of their own, whose only power comes in the grace of the gospel of Jesus Christ. In the Christian story, we're different from "the rulers of the Gentiles" who "lord it over them" (Mt 20:25), because we serve the one who "did not come to be served, but to serve, and to give his life as a ransom for many (Mt 20:28). The Christian happy ending is not the glory of the empire but the assured victory of the resurrected Jesus, whose coming kingdom undoes the power of Rome. Early Christians believed in a story that recognized God as more important than Caesar. They told that story with their bodies by practicing radical chastity for both women *and* men, and they believed that chastity was to be lived out in celibate singleness or fidelity in marriage.

This chastity was a sign of the true story of God's faithfulness to God's people. As the God of Israel is faithful to the people of Israel, as Jesus the bridegroom is faithful to the church as bride, Christian men and women display God's radical faithfulness with their bodies. Celibate singleness was not a thing in Rome, but it became a thing for Christians who wanted their bodies to be for God, not for the state or the men with power. Male chastity was not a thing in Rome, but it became a thing for Christians who knew that God uses the weak things of this world to shame the strong. Thinking of married women as persons instead of baby makers was not a thing in Rome, but it was a new possibility for Christians, who knew that women are not possessions but are daughters of the King. Many Christians were slaves, victims of ongoing sexual abuse. And honor for those slaves was not a thing in Rome, who were discounted as victims of fate. But honor for slaves was the gospel truth for Christians, who knew that the value of every human lies in being loved by God, and not in whether or not their bodies are "pure" or "manly." Slaves endured sexual assault, but they were not broken teacups. They were beloved sons and daughters of the King.

Our world looks different from ancient Rome, but it isn't without its own version of sexual ethics driven by a story about sexual freedom and pleasure as central human goods. I hope to show the differences between our world's stories and the Christian story by considering a number of questions about Christians and sex and showing how Christian answers to those questions fit with the gospel story.

SEX OUTSIDE OF MARRIAGE?

Let's start with a classic. Should Christians have sex outside of marriage? No. Marriage is the space of vowed covenant faithfulness, and so it is the only place where sex can tell the story of God's covenant faithfulness to us. Christians don't reject sex outside of marriage because we don't like sex. In fact, Scripture is clear that sex is a good gift, given to us by our Creator and not to be rejected. We also don't reject sex outside of marriage because we want to control our children. In fact, Christianity requires that parents give up ultimate control over our children (something that parents can never really have anyway, though many of us like to cling to an illusion of it!) and trust our children to God. And we don't reject sex outside of marriage because we think we're pure while the world outside of us is impure. In fact, Christians are clear that we can have no purity outside of Christ, that we, like every human being who has ever lived, are broken sinners in need of a Savior. The teacup view of sexuality denies our fundamental brokenness and turns sexual purity into a kind of innocence that Christians don't actually believe exists and a kind of works righteousness Christians don't believe is possible. We don't reject sex outside of marriage in an attempt to preserve our purity or to earn some kind of gold stars with God.

We reject sex outside of marriage because marriage is a story about God's covenant faithfulness to God's people. In marriage we make public covenant promises—vows—to be faithful to this one other person, faithful no matter what ("for better or worse, richer or poorer, in sickness and health"), faithful unto death. We promise to love and care for this person through thick and thin, and that promise is made in the context of the body of Christ. We promise that this person, and only this person, is the one with whom we will seal that promise with our bodies.

MARRIAGE AND THE GOOD GIFT OF SEX

Christian marriage is a sign of Jesus' faithfulness to and one flesh unity with his church. Paul expands on this metaphor—which is found throughout Scripture—in his letter to the Ephesians. He instructs husbands and wives to mutual, self-giving love for one another and describes marriage as, "a great mystery, and I am applying it to Christ and the church" (Eph 5:32 NRSV).

Christians haven't always been clear that our sexual ethics is about telling the story of God's faithfulness. Unfortunately, we've often reduced it to a set of legalistic rules, or we've implicitly embraced others' stories as the ones we want to tell with our bodies.

This makes it difficult for some Christians to embrace sex as a good thing. Sex is a gift from a God, a good creation made by a good Creator for good purposes, but when Christians have spent years thinking about sex in legalistic terms, it can be difficult to embrace this good in marriage. The precious teacup view of sexuality assumes that sex breaks the teacup. It makes sex into an impurity, a destroyer. I talk to Christians who feel fear or disgust around sex. They've believed stories about sex that would make it about humans earning purity instead of about faithfulness, and so when they marry they have trouble embracing sex as a good. Embracing the good gift of sex can also be difficult for those of us who have been victims of sexual violence, who have experienced the ways that sinful humans can take something good and twist it, using it for evil. Fortunately, marriage is for the long term, and provides plenty of time and space to learn to embrace the good gift of sexuality. And as the context of vowed covenant faithfulness, marriage ought to be the place where two spouses can patiently and tenderly do this learning, bathing it in prayer.

DATING, DESIRE, AND SEXUAL FAITHFULNESS

I talk to many Christians who are dating and who struggle to maintain the boundaries of sexual faithfulness. This isn't all bad. Desire is a powerful thing, and that power has to do with the goodness of our bodies and of sexuality as created by God. God made human beings amazingly beautiful, deeply attractive. Desire isn't bad, but it does have to be channeled (and this is as true for married Christians as it is for unmarried ones!). The gospel story is about channeling our desire, through marriage or through singleness, toward God. Desire isn't bad, but desire needs to be ordered rightly, and Christian faith should help us with that ordering. We're called to channel desire toward God in embodied holiness as a way to bear witness to the God who loves us faithfully.

So, if an unmarried Christian couple wants to maintain sexual boundaries, because they believe sex belongs in marriage where it can tell the story of God's faithfulness, how can they do so? There's a tendency in Christian dating advice to avoid clear advice around these questions, to provide general principles instead of practical instructions. I get that. Those principles matter, and practical instructions can seem legalistic or culturally relative, but in my experience, people really need practical advice, so I'm going to hazard some. It won't be perfect, and other Christians may have good reasons for offering different advice, but here's mine: keep your clothes on.

Clothes are actually pretty significant in the Christian story. They come into the story after Adam and Eve fall into sin. Where before they'd enjoyed unashamed, safe, naked intimacy in Eden, a world of sin requires boundaries and protections, and God doesn't leave them with only the sad little leaves they've tried to use to cover their nakedness. God provides "garments of skin" (Gen 3:21) as an act of loving care for people who now have to make their way in a sinful world.

Marriage, when it's holy and healthy, ought to be a little bit like the Garden of Eden before the fall: a safe place to get naked. Outside of marriage, I suggest you keep your clothes on. Christians will sometimes set the boundary of sexual intimacy outside of marriage so that only intercourse is off the table. This strikes me as quite legalistic and a deeply problematic way of trying to tell the story of God's faithfulness. If you keep your clothes on, you won't have to navigate ever intensifying levels of sexual intimacy, all while desperately trying to avoid intercourse. You'll know where to stop.

Some Christian dating advice has so emphasized "purity" that it discourages any kind of physical intimacy, even a kiss, outside of marriage. I worry that this route can carry with it a dangerous sense that sex itself is bad or dirty, rather than being a good thing that needs to be rightly ordered toward God. I also worry it can carry a misunderstanding about desire, as though it were wrong to long for another person, as though desire needs to be wiped out instead of ordered toward God. It seems to me that some good kissing, and the wanting that goes with that, makes good sense in a relationship in which two people are discerning whether they will one day marry and one day enjoy full physical intimacy, which is a good gift from God and a beautiful sign of God's faithfulness in union with us.

THE CHRISTIAN STORY AND SEXUAL SIN

In our contemporary world's story about sexuality, there is almost no such thing as sexual sin. Everything is considered permissible because desire isn't for God, desire is for pleasure, desire is for me. If Christianity isn't antisex, then how does it define sexual sin? We tend to think of it as a laundry list of forbidden acts, but Scripture gives us a bigger picture.

Sexual sin tells false stories about God and the world. The New Testament uses the word *porneia* to talk about this kind of sin. In English it's usually translated "fornication," but this is a cold, clinical word. We're not sure what "fornication" is supposed to describe or whether it has anything to do with the world we live in. For this reason, I'm just going to use the Greek *porneia* to try to give a sense of its implications. *Porneia* is a word with broad meaning; it points to any kind of sexual sin that would violate the exclusive covenant faithfulness of marriage. *Porneia* is sex outside of marriage, but it's also sex that exploits or disregards the precious humanity of another. *Porneia* is adultery. *Porneia* is abuse. In the world of the New Testament, the word *porneia* was associated with prostitution, an institution that was almost the equivalent of slavery. *Porneia* is sex that is bought and sold, sex that exploits human beings, sex that denies the precious humanity of another. *Porneia* is the opposite of holy, healthy married sex, which is freely given and freely received, in mutuality and covenant faithfulness.

Rejecting *porneia* has always been part of Christian teaching and identity. The rejection of *porneia* is part of what made it clear, in the ancient world, that Christians worship the one God. In the book of Acts, early Christian leaders were dealing with questions about what it would mean for Gentiles (non-Jews) to convert to Christ. Would these Gentile Christians need to obey the whole of Jewish law? Through the power of the Holy Spirit the church discerned that Gentile Christians would not be held to the whole law: "For it has seemed good to the Holy Spirit and to us to impose on you no further burden than these essentials: that you abstain from what has been sacrificed to idols and from blood and from what is strangled and from *porneia*. If you keep yourselves from these, you will do well" (Acts 15:28-29 NRSV). What does abstaining from food sacrificed to idols have in common with abstaining from *porneia*? Both kinds of abstaining tell a story about absolute devotion to the one God of Israel, the Father of our Lord Jesus Christ. Abstaining from food sacrificed to idols denies power and reality to those idols. Abstaining from *porneia* denies that our bodies are for pleasure, power, or the state of Rome. Our bodies are for God.

It's important that *porneia* shares a root with our word *pornography*. Pornography is a form of *porneia* that is incredibly rampant in our world. Pornography shares many important features with some of the biblical accounts of *porneia*. Like the prostitution of enslaved persons in the ancient world, the contemporary pornography industry exploits vulnerable human beings with few resources or protections. Sometimes, that contemporary industry literally exploits trafficked persons, contemporary slaves. And tropes and themes that are prevalent in pornography denigrate human beings, especially women, and make sex about power, performance, and control instead of mutual joy in covenant faithfulness. Increasingly, it seems that the prevalence of pornography makes people think that tropes used in porn are normal and healthy. I would encourage Christians to keep the artifacts of pornography, both watching and using porn itself and imitating porn's scripts and tropes, out of our bedrooms.

In 1 Thessalonians, we read more about the importance of rejecting *porneia*:

> This is the will of God, your sanctification: that you abstain from fornication; that each one of you know how to control your own body in holiness and honor, not with lustful passion, like the Gentiles who do not know God; that no one wrong or exploit a brother or sister in this matter, because the Lord is an avenger in all these things, just as we have already told you beforehand and solemnly warned you. For God did not call us to impurity but in holiness. Therefore whoever rejects this rejects not human authority but God, who also gives his Holy Spirit to you. (1 Thess 4:3-8 NRSV)

But how is it possible to abstain from *porneia*? Sexual sin has a powerful draw. The key here is in the last verse of this passage, where Paul tells us that this is not from "human authority" but from God, "who also gives his Holy Spirit to you" (v. 8). The rejection of *porneia* is possible because the power of the Holy Spirit goes with us. It's not something Christians are supposed to be able to do by our own strength and power. We don't desperately try to make ourselves holy. We don't earn purity. We can only begin to reject *porneia* because the Spirit, who is God, indwells us and will give us divine power to control our bodies "in holiness and honor."

Sexual holiness is not possible by our human strength, but it does become possible because we become part of God's new creation in Christ Jesus. In Corinthians, Paul lists *porneia* alongside other sins (some sexual, some otherwise), and he writes to his fellow believers that "this is what some of you used to be."

But that is not the end of the story. Paul knows that Christian faith doesn't stop with what we used to be. It moves us forward, allowing us to use our bodies to tell the true story of God's faithfulness in Jesus Christ, through the power of the Holy Spirit; "But you were washed, you were sanctified, you were justified in the name of the Lord Jesus Christ and by the Spirit of our God" (1 Cor 6:11). All our sin, sexual sin absolutely included, is washed away in the blood of Jesus, and the power to live a new life is ours because the Spirit of God indwells us. We will have to rely on the Spirit day by day, moment by moment, as we seek to tell God's story with our bodies. And when we fail, when we sin, when we tell false stories with our bodies, God is there offering forgiveness and healing. We were never "pure," so there's no purity for us to "lose" when we sin sexually. But there is purity to be gained, in union with Christ, by the power of the Spirit.

SINGLENESS, MARRIAGE, AND CHRISTIAN FAITHFULNESS

If we're going to use our bodies to tell the story of God's faithfulness, then we need to find ways to honor and rejoice in celibate singleness, and, sadly, this is a task many contemporary Christian communities are failing at miserably. For much of Christian history, celibate singleness was honored as a high calling, following the example of Jesus. While marriage divides our interests and makes us "anxious about the affairs of the world," single Christians can use their bodies to tell the story of "unhindered devotion to the Lord" (1 Cor 7:33-35 NRSV). Scripture and Christian history greatly honor singleness.

Both faithful marriage and faithful singleness are ways of telling the world about God's faithfulness. Both kinds of faithfulness deny that sex is the ultimate good and that humans need unfettered sexual pleasure to live a good life. Both kinds of faithfulness point to a God who is bigger and more beautiful and more desirable than the desire for another human being could be. Both point to a purpose beyond this life. Both mirror the steadfast love of a God who loves us no matter what, who never turns away from us despite our unfaithfulness. And both are possible only by the grace of that God.

If we're going to tell such a radical, countercultural story with our bodies, we'll need a lot to sustain us. We won't be able to do this alone. The courage, strength, and endurance required to embrace sexual faithfulness aren't something we can dig out of our own willpower. We're broken sinners, after all, and we'll need God's sustaining and empowering grace for this journey. God provides that grace in numerous ways, including through prayer, work, community, and the worshiping life of the church.

The whole of Christian discipleship, including sexual discipleship, grows in and through prayer. As beloved sons and daughters of the King, made one with the Father through Jesus, the Holy Spirit dwells within us, enabling us to pray even when we don't have the right words: "Likewise the Spirit helps us in our weakness; for we do not know how to pray as we ought, but that very Spirit intercedes with sighs too deep for words" (Rom 8:26 NRSV). The indwelling Spirit, helping us to pray, is the one who "raised Jesus from the dead" and who will also "give life to" our "mortal bodies" (Rom 8:11 NRSV). The Spirit's work of giving life to our bodies includes the power for sexual holiness, the power to tell the story of God's faithfulness. As we seek that life, we will have to turn in prayer to our loving Father, moment by moment and day by day.

Human beings aren't brains on sticks. We're embodied souls, embodied wholes, and to thrive, we need good work to do with our bodies. For married people, enjoying sexual intimacy is part of that work. For single people, chastity is made possible partly because they too have good work to do with their bodies. We all need to use our bodies to do good things. We all need to use our bodies for love. This work includes the stuff we normally think of as "work": whatever we get paid to do, the chores that have to be done around the home, the reading and studying of the student life. But it also includes wonderful, embodied work that lets us use our bodies for Jesus and the people Jesus loves, work that goes beyond our narrower definitions of work: painting, baking, exercise, walking the dog, playing games, visiting the sick and imprisoned, caring for children in the church nursery or teaching Sunday school, and so on.

Humans weren't designed to live alone, and we need one another for accountability and support for sexual faithfulness as for every area of discipleship. This is why marriage is a public covenant, made in front of friends, family, and the church community. Married faithfulness needs the support of the community. Single faithfulness is the same, but the structures of our culture mean we may have to look hard for that communal support. We can find God's grace and power for faithfulness in accountability partners, small group support, friends and mentors, and the larger structures of the church. For both married and single Christians, we also need the community of the body of Christ to sustain us in relationships. No spouse can fill all of our relational needs, and no single Christian should have to go at it alone. We all need shared meals, shared nights out, laughter, and friendship. We also need to come together to worship and to the Lord's table, which are two important sites of community where God has promised to give us grace.

Finally, we will need an ongoing relationship with God to sustain us as we seek sexual holiness. No Christian, no human being, is sexually innocent, and every one of us will need to continually turn to God for forgiveness and healing. There is no lost or broken or given up in the realm of sexuality that is beyond God's ability to find, to redeem, and to restore. Because sexuality, like every area of human life, is an area where sin will continue to tempt and infect us, the process of healing and of growing into holy sexuality will be a lifelong one, one where we will learn to turn again and again to God's mercy and renewal.

Ultimately, sexuality is about doing one of the most exciting things we get to do as Christians. It is about obeying the command to "glorify God in your body" (1 Cor 6:20 NRSV) and testifying to the truth and power of the gospel story. The good news about sex is that God made it as a good gift, a gift that allows for deep intimacy and unity in marriage and that rejoices in the beauty of human being as created by God. The good news about sex is that God allows us to use our sexual bodies to tell God's story, the story of God's faithfulness. The good news about sex is that no sexual sin can put us beyond the love of God, and that God is there to offer forgiveness and healing and to enable us to tell the world the truth about who he is. We aren't fragile teacups. Instead, we "have this treasure in clay jars, so that it may be made clear that this extraordinary power belongs to God and does not come from us" (2 Cor 4:7 NRSV).

Chapter Five

Marriage

MARGARET KIM PETERSON

A FEW WEEKS INTO THE SEMESTER A STUDENT raised a question. Why had this class on Christian marriage not yet included a list of principles which, if faithfully applied, would result reliably in a successful Christian marriage? Every other talk or sermon or weekend workshop on Christian relationships to which this young person had been exposed had included a list of such principles. "They never work," he admitted. "But I still want them."

Isn't this the story of our lives? On the one hand, we want a recipe, a formula that we can cling to that will bring us safely and predictably through the perils of life. On the other hand, we know that's not how it works. The Christian life is not a set of principles to be applied. The Christian life is a story to be lived. And that story is neither safe nor predictable. Just ask the Gospel writers, whose stories all include both crucifixion and resurrection.

In the decades after that student asked his question, I taught the marriage class many more times. In the beginning, my coteacher was my husband and faculty colleague. He taught New Testament, I taught theology, and together we collaborated on the marriage class. By the end, I had spent years juggling work, parenting and caring for a dying spouse, and was now a widowed single mother.

Among my companions along this not-safe, not-predictable life course were the students who took the marriage class. Together, we grappled with our shared wishes for things to be simpler than they were, while doing our best to come to grips with things as they actually are: things like love and loss, faith and family, peace and conflict, sex and children, marriage and singleness, widowhood and divorce.

I never made a list of principles. But over the years I did accumulate a collection of myths. That seems like the right word to describe a range of notions that came up again and again in class as students talked about their hopes and fears and the sometimes not-so-wise words they had received from one or another quarter. These always proved great jumping-off points for conversation. So in honor of every student who has ever wanted a list, here is a top ten list not of principles but of myths.

MYTH 1: IF YOU DON'T GET MARRIED, YOU'RE DOOMED

"I think most Christians believe that singleness is not an option for Christians, either as a way to serve God or as a way to be happy."

We live in a culture that privileges marriage and married persons. United States law grants dozens of benefits to married partners, ranging from inheritance rights to access to spousal health insurance coverage to preferred visa status to hospital visitation privileges. Churches build centers for marriage and family life and segregate single people into groups whose primary purpose often seems to be matchmaking. And sex is framed by many Christians as the best thing ever, provided you wait until you're married to have it.

It has not always been so. From very early in the Christian era, most Christians understood marriage as an acceptable but not ideal choice. Jesus was unmarried, so far as we know, and is recorded as having portrayed marriage as a temporal but not an eternal entity (Lk 20:34-36). The apostle Paul, who was also unmarried, suggests in 1 Corinthians 7 that singleness may in fact be preferable to marriage.

Certain passages of the New Testament also seem to suggest that there are two ways to live the Christian life. There is a basic way that involves obeying God's commandments—refraining from murder or covetousness or adultery, for example. And then there is a higher way

that involves not just the commandments but also the "counsels"—
that is, ideals like nonviolence and voluntary poverty and celibacy
(Mt 5:38-40; 19:12, 21). The commandments apply equally to everyone;
the counsels—early Christians thought—are higher ethical requirements that may be assumed voluntarily by some.

Primarily on the basis of this distinction between commands and
counsels, the church as a whole eventually came to esteem virginity
over marriage. Christians understood matrimony as a good way to be
obedient to God, but celibacy, they thought, was a better way to be holy.
By "celibacy," they did not mean simply the state of being unmarried
or sexually abstinent. Celibacy was a vowed state akin to matrimony,
only in this case the vow was not a vow of marriage but a vow of perpetual virginity for the sake of the kingdom of God, a vow that was to
be lived out not in a private home but in a monastery or convent or in
the priestly life.

This changed dramatically in the sixteenth century, at least in those
parts of Europe that were touched by the Protestant Reformation.
Protestants dismantled the theological framework that had supported
celibacy, arguing that the ability to keep a vow of perpetual virginity
was a gift given to a few, not a law that the church could or should
impose on whole classes of persons, like parish priests. Matrimony, not
celibacy, was the normal vocation of most people. Pastors, in particular,
should be free to marry; the pastor's home and family (not, as formerly,
the cloister) was now envisioned as a kind of outpost of heaven on earth.

What did not develop at the time of the Reformation, and has not
developed in the centuries since, is a robust theology of singleness. The
Protestant Reformers reclaimed the goodness of marriage, but without
considering the alternative—that is, the condition of persons bound
neither by a vow of matrimony nor a vow of celibacy, persons living
neither as a partner in a married-couple-headed household nor in a
religious community under obedience to a superior. People, in other
words, who are single.

Hence, perhaps, the feeling of doom on the part of Christian young
people contemplating the possibility of ongoing singleness. Singleness

is uncharted territory, both theologically and ecclesially. The church has never made marriage a law. Christians are, technically, free to marry or not to marry. But if there is no recognition within the church that singleness is a normal condition for an adult, just how free are Christians to remain single?

The truth is that singleness is a perfectly acceptable way to be both an adult and a Christian. This is good news. We all start out single. Many of us remain single well into adulthood, and even more of us become single again. Are there challenges to the single life? Of course there are. And if you'd really rather be married, you may not feel much like rising to the challenges of singleness. But the problem there is not with singleness per se but with the distance between what you want and what you have. That is a whole different conversation.

MYTH 2: IF YOUR PARENTS HAVE SET A POOR EXAMPLE FOR YOU, YOU'RE DOOMED

"When I look at my parents, I wonder what is keeping them together. If this is what marriage is, I don't want it."

Just because people get married doesn't mean their marriage will flourish. And the children of empty or conflict-ridden marriages often end up wondering: what is the point? Marriage can seem like an undertaking in which some make it and some don't, and you may be afraid that you will be among those who don't, that you will end up miserable or divorced, or maybe both.

Divorce is first mentioned in Christian Scripture in the book of Deuteronomy, where it is assumed that divorce takes place and an effort is made to regulate some of the circumstances surrounding it (Deut 24:1-4). In the New Testament Jesus takes issue with the notion that a man should be able easily to divorce his wife and marry another (Mk 10:2-12; Mt 5:31-32; 19:3-9; Lk 16:16-18). And the apostle Paul suggests that under some circumstances a Christian believer may divorce an unbelieving spouse (1 Cor 7:10-16).

Jesus' emphasis on the intended permanence of marriage led Christians in the early centuries of the church to conclude that Christian marriage, unlike marriage under the old covenant, was in its very nature indissoluble. Husbands and wives were bound to each other as long as they both lived, and "divorce" could mean only separation, with no right to remarry for either spouse, no matter what had happened in the marriage. Only if a marriage were annulled—that is, determined by a church court never to have existed at all—was remarriage a possibility.

The Protestant Reformers disagreed, asserting that under certain circumstances—adultery, life-threatening violence, abandonment—a Christian marriage could be dissolved, leaving at least one of the parties free to remarry during the former spouse's lifetime. And they moved the adjudication of marriage and divorce cases from the ecclesiastical courts to the civil courts, thus opening the door to the possibility of civil divorce as it exists today.

Which brings us back to the reality reflected in the book of Deuteronomy, which is this: people get divorced. People of faith get divorced. People who entered into their marriages with every good intention find themselves in situations in which divorce seems like the least bad of the available options. And if religious or secular authorities permit it, they may in fact divorce, not because they are bad people but because they are doing the best they can.

If your parents are divorced or their marriage is so miserable or destructive that it might have been better if they had divorced or not married in the first place, you may well wonder if it is really possible for you to do better. As you consider your hopes and fears, something to keep in mind might be the continuities between marriage and Christian life in general. Paul identifies some of those things as the "fruit of the Spirit": love, joy, peace, patience, kindness, goodness, faithfulness, gentleness, and self-control (Gal 5:22-23).

These qualities are to characterize all Christians, married or single. In this sense, being married is not all that different from being single. Christians, whether married or not, are called to be faithful and loving and willing to follow Christ into both crucifixion and resurrection. Does cultivation of these qualities guarantee success in marriage or anything else? Of course not. Life is not like that. But when Christian spouses work individually and together to cultivate the fruit of the Spirit, their hopes of building a healthy and sustainable marital partnership become less an impossible dream and more a reasonable expectation.

MYTH 3: THE BEST WAY TO MANAGE CONFLICT IS TO ASSIGN DECISION-MAKING POWER TO ONE SPOUSE

"At home and at church, I was taught that Ephesians 5 meant that if there was a disagreement about a decision that needed to be made, the man made it. The woman's voice could be heard and considered, but the man in the relationship should make the final decision."

Conflict is an inevitable component of human relationships. People are not all the same, and they have different ideas about what to do, how to do it, and whether it is a good idea to be doing it at all. Some conflicts may be trivial. Should the toothpaste tube be squeezed from the bottom or from the top? But trivial matters can become the battlegrounds on which we act out more significant differences that lie beneath the surface.

Sometimes these deeper conflicts remain unaddressed simply because we have not realized they are there. Surface-level conflicts can become invitations and opportunities to dig a little deeper and to try to figure out what is going on. But sometimes we are hesitant to identify or address deeper differences precisely because they are nontrivial. We are afraid that if we look at them, they will engulf and destroy the relationship.

Is there a way to guarantee that this will never happen? Enter Ephesians 5. This is understood by some Christians as assigning decision-making power in any male-female intimate relationship to the man. The appeal of this arrangement is that it seems to promise relationships in which conflict is resolved instantaneously and automatically. As soon as a husband and wife (or boyfriend and girlfriend) suspect they might not be able to agree, the woman steps aside, the man makes the decision, and the conflict evaporates.

Among the problems with this interpretation of Ephesians 5 (and they are legion) are two in particular: it does not work in practice, and it is fatally flawed in theory. Even when people articulate these ideals, they often do not live up to them. And more fundamentally, to read this passage in this way is to affirm that Christian marriage is at its heart an ideology of power and control. If this were true, it would certainly not be an attractive brief in favor of marriage.

In fact, it is not true. In 1 Corinthians 11:3, the apostle Paul points to God the Father and Jesus Christ as the model for Christian spouses in this regard, and it is most emphatically not the case that God the Father is in the business of making decisions on behalf of the Holy Trinity when the Father and the Son are unable to reach agreement in any other way.

On the contrary, the relationship between the Father and the Son is characterized by perfect peace and mutuality. And so should the relationship between Christian spouses be one of mutuality. The challenge is that this takes time. It takes effort. It takes a willingness to talk and to listen for long enough that it can become clear what the issues are, what the feelings and desires of both spouses are, and what some possible plans of action might be.

Simply assigning decision-making power to one spouse can seem a lot quicker and easier. Husband and wife don't really even have to work together. He does his job and decides, she does her job and goes along, and they're done. And that is exactly the problem. They haven't actually dealt with their differences. They've just done an end run around them. They are no more united when they are done than they were when they began. There has got to be a better way.

MYTH 4: THE BEST WAY TO MANAGE CONFLICT IS TO IGNORE IT AND HOPE FOR THE BEST

"In my relationship I find myself not wanting to disagree, thinking that will promote unity and togetherness. So even when I see a problem, I let it fester, assuming it will somehow work itself out and disappear with no harm done.

I can't say I've ever seen that happen with any remotely serious matter, but somehow the belief remains."

Alas, conflict avoidance is not conflict resolution, as all those of us who have tried it know. So what alternatives are there to handing decision-making authority to one spouse ahead of time? One possibility is egalitarianism or the affirmation that husbands and wives should have equal regard for one another and an equal say in what happens in their marriage. This has in its favor that it does not stack the deck against one spouse in favor of the other and instead encourages partners to encounter each other as equals.

Unfortunately, egalitarianism shares a major drawback with the one-spouse-is-in-charge model, and that is that both are much more about the distribution of power than they are about collaboration. Both models too often see relationships between marital partners as a zero-sum game in which power held by one spouse can only come at the expense of power held by the other. The only question is whether power is to be distributed evenly or unevenly.

A better question is, how can spouses learn not just to compete with one another but actually to work together? Think teamwork, not competition. When two people play on the same sports team, they are working together toward a shared goal. They pursue tactical strategies that showcase each other's strengths and set each other up to succeed. Most important of all, they practice and practice and practice, because any sport is the most fun when you play it often and well.

The same is true of relationships and of the relational work—or play—that is involved in meeting the challenges posed by differences within the relationship or by stressors outside the relationship. No one is born knowing how to handle stress or conflict. These are things we have to learn. We learn in our families, we learn in our childhood friendships, and we need to continue learning as we move into and through adult relationships like marriage.

Successful conflict management is often much less about resolving conflict than it is about the process by which conflict is addressed. Some conflicts don't call for resolution. If you're fighting because you're both overtired, don't make a decision; take a nap. Some conflicts cannot be resolved or may resurface periodically over the lifetime of a relationship. If one of you likes to act quickly and decisively and the other likes to take time to reflect, don't criticize each other for being the wrong sort of person; take a deep breath and bring both of your skill sets to the problem at hand.

Most of all, work to build consensus. This may not be a familiar practice. Our culture is so individualistic that it can be hard to imagine there can be a greater good than getting what you want, or at least as much of it as you can manage. But working with your partner to identify or create possibilities that will be positive for both of you can be far more satisfying than simply trying to split your differences.

MYTH 5: PREMARITAL "PURITY" HAS ALWAYS BEEN AT THE HEART OF A TRADITIONAL CHRISTIAN SEXUAL ETHIC

"I was taught that sex before marriage was pretty much the worst possible thing you could do. I mean, we were taught that murder was very wrong, but obviously we would never do that, so sex before marriage was probably the worst thing we could ever do."

Where premarital sex is seen as the worst possible sin, there premarital "purity" will be seen as the most fundamental virtue. This is a modern phenomenon. Historically, Christian tradition identified procreation as the fundamental purpose of sex. Nonprocreative sexual activity was understood as a "sin against nature" and as inherently worse than any form of procreative sexual activity. Thus, according to a traditional (medieval) Christian sexual ethic, masturbation is considered a worse sin than adultery, precisely because adultery is potentially procreative and masturbation is not.

According to that same traditional Christian sexual ethic, the most fundamental sexual virtue was fidelity to one's vows. For a monk or a nun, this meant fidelity to a vow of celibacy, meaning not merely premarital virginity but perpetual virginity for the sake of the kingdom of God. For a married person, it meant fidelity to a vow of matrimony, meaning a promise to engage only in procreative sexual relations, and only with one's spouse.

As for the sexual activity of persons not under vows, well, the focus of the church has mostly been elsewhere. Premarital sex is formally against the rules, but it is and has always been common. In agrarian societies like those of the Middle Ages, when families depended on children for labor, premarital pregnancy was seen by many young people and their parents as a kind of insurance policy, allowing couples to know before marriage that their union was fertile.

Records of marriages and births in eighteenth- and nineteenth-century America show that a large proportion of first births were to parents who either were not married or who had married fewer than nine months before the birth of the child. Closer to our own time, an analysis of data gathered between 1982 and 2002 has shown that in that period, by age twenty about 75 percent of Americans had had premarital sex, and by age forty-four 95 percent had done so.[1]

The bottom line is this: many, many brides and grooms, throughout the history of the world and of the church, have been sexually experienced, often with each other, before they got to the altar. Premarital virginity is a good thing, and there are good reasons, both theological and practical, to hold it up as an ideal and to strive for it in practice. But it is not and never has been the usual pattern, in the sense of being the actual experience of most individuals or couples.

"But Dr. Peterson! Are you giving us permission to have premarital sex?" No, I am not giving anyone permission to have premarital sex. People are already having premarital sex without my permission. Ninety-five percent of the country is having premarital sex without my permission. Clearly, they're not waiting for my permission. What I am doing is telling the truth about what people are actually doing.

But if they shouldn't be doing it, wouldn't it be better to silently gloss over that fact—or perhaps even actively cover it up—for fear of encouraging more bad behavior? No, I don't think so. I think Christian faith does better when it acknowledges openly and nondefensively the realities of people's lives. Not everybody agrees with me about this. But in my judgment the way to have a potentially useful conversation about anything is to tell the truth. That includes the truth about our sexual lives and the ways they do or do not conform to traditionally Christian ideals.

MYTH 6: PREMARITAL "PURITY" IS THE ROYAL ROAD TO SEXUAL SATISFACTION IN MARRIAGE

"I was led to believe that if you remained abstinent before marriage, there would be a huge reward waiting for you in the bedroom once you got married. You would have an instantaneously pleasurable and successful sex life. The wedding night would be the most amazing night of your life, and it if wasn't, the only reason could be that there was something wrong with you or with your relationship."

Here again we see the vast gulf that lies between a traditional Christian sexual ethic and the ethic of premarital "purity." For the vast majority of the church's life, sexual pleasure was seen as a problem, not a goal. Moral theologians fretted over the fact that even the most well-intentioned husbands and wives, engaged in sexual relations with one another purely out of obedience to God and a wish to conceive and bring forth children in response to God's command, might experience a degree of pleasure that might tempt them to cross the line into the territory of lust and thus of sin.

In our day, Christians have mostly changed their minds about this. Sex—including married sex—is understood as properly involving sensuality and pleasure. But if pleasure is a goal of sex, the last way to get there is the ethic of premarital "purity." The anxiety, fear, shame, and ignorance around sexuality and embodiment that are deployed as primary motivators within purity culture do not automatically evaporate on the wedding night or any night thereafter.

On the contrary, young people whose sexual formation has been limited to not knowing, not doing, not feeling, and not experiencing themselves as sexual beings arrive at the threshold of married sexuality woefully unprepared at best and at worst guilt-ridden, terrified, and dissociated. Sexual pain is not uncommon and is interpreted not as a treatable medical and psychological problem but as evidence of spiritual inadequacy and failure.

It doesn't have to be this way. Everyone is a sexual person, and adequate sexual formation acknowledges this and considers how both single and married persons can live fully into themselves as embodied and sexual beings. You can grow into an experience of your adult sexuality that is positive and energizing. And if you marry, you can make the transition to married life and married sexuality knowing that the wedding night may or may not be *amazing*, and that's just fine.

And you can expect your sexual relationship with your spouse to change over time, from the goodness of youth to the goodness of maturity. Sex is about relationship and vulnerability and openness to intimacy. These aspects of marriage can become better and better with age, and as a result, maturing couples can find their sexual satisfaction increasing as the years go by. Sexuality and sensuality can remain valuable elements of your marriage through the seasons of your life together.

MYTH 7: MARRIAGE IS EASY

"I walked down the aisle with the expectation that I would live the rest of my life in a fairy-tale world in which I would always be adored, cherished, and loved. My husband would never disagree with me because I would always be right. If an issue did arise, we would settle it by talking for hours over coffee, never raising our voices or getting frustrated with one another. We would conclude our conversation with a hug and a kiss while thanking one another for the brilliant perspective. Then we would go home and make love."

It is natural to have expectations of marriage. People get married in part because they expect that certain desirable things will happen if they do. Some expectations make life easier, by helping us to know what to look for, priming us to be grateful for good things when they occur, and preparing us to meet challenges when they arise. Other expectations make life harder, by encouraging us to want the impossible and setting us up for inevitable disappointment when the impossible does not, in fact, transpire.

If you get married expecting a fairy tale—if you expect that your relationship will reach perfection the moment you say "I do" and that everything thereafter will be a kind of static "happily ever after"—you will be disappointed. Fortunately, real life is a lot more interesting than that. In real life the wedding is the beginning of all kinds of adventures. Your marriage now has the opportunity to grow from small beginnings into maturity, even as a seed grows into a flower or a tree.

It is realistic to expect that the process of getting to know your partner will continue after you are married. This is true no matter how well you know each other when you marry. The commitment that marriage represents makes it possible for spouses to perceive one another and to reveal themselves to one another in new and deeper ways. This will be more interesting and complex and challenging than you might have imagined, and it will require effort on both of your parts.

It is realistic to expect other kinds of change as well. No one stands still in life; no relationship can remain unchanged over time. The question is not whether your marriage will change but how it will change. Many of these changes may not be either good or bad but simply different—for example, those that will come with the growth of your children, should you be blessed with them, from infancy through childhood and adolescence and into adulthood. Each of these stages brings its own challenges and its own joys, and your privilege as spouses is to encounter these stages and changes together.

Of course, it is possible for people to change in ways that make them less rather than more able to live peaceably and contentedly together. If you want to change together in ways that are increasingly positive and interrelated, you have to cultivate community. You will have to live and work and play with each other and with your children and extended families and neighbors and friends, and in this way build a network of relationships that can help to make your marriage a success and a joy.

MYTH 8: MARRIAGE IS HARD

"Everyone is constantly telling me that marriage is difficult and hard work. It really frightens me because, so far, I am enjoying every minute of it. I find

myself waiting for the bad times to come, thinking that it will be any day now. Is it really going to get as bad and difficult as people say it is? Should I prepare myself for the worst?"

When people say marriage is hard, what do they mean? Do they mean that marriage is hard compared to other paths in life that are not hard (like singleness, presumably)? If this is what they mean, they're wrong. Marriage is not a quick way to make your life miserable. It is not a burden that you could have avoided by remaining single but that you must now do your best to bear up under. Marriage and singleness are different paths in life. There are benefits and drawbacks to either path, but neither one is by definition easier or harder than the other.

On the other hand, marriage is hard in the sense that becoming really good at anything is hard. Anyone who plays a sport or an instrument well can tell you it takes a lot of work. But good athletes and good musicians are willing to work that hard for that long because they value what they are doing and they want to do it well. That love and that goal make the process as a whole a welcome discipline, even through seasons when it may feel like a long, slow slog.

So also with marriage. Sometimes marital partners are so enchanted by each other that it is easy to listen patiently, to speak gently, to look for ways to serve one another and to please one another. And then there are times when none of those things seems easy, when it requires a great deal of discipline to continue to practice the art of treating one another with consideration, honesty, and respect. This is hard work; so yes, in this sense marriage is hard.

There is a second sense in which marriage is hard: it is hard because life is hard. Marriage, like life, is interwoven with loss and bounded by death. This is why Christian marriage vows read as they do: "I take you as my wedded spouse, for better, for worse, for richer, for poorer, in sickness and in health, to love and to cherish, until we are parted by death." Christian marriage is not a gamble whereby we hope that if we choose this person, everything will be perfect forever. Christian marriage is a promise to love one another in the midst of whatever life brings—and recognizing too that we do not have all the time in the world, because death comes to all of us.

We are invited, therefore, to make the most of every day, bearing together whatever burdens come to us. One or both of you may bring losses with you into marriage—perhaps the premature death of a parent or of a sibling. You may encounter losses in your early married life—a move for work or school that takes you far from family, a miscarriage or a struggle with infertility.

Later life may bring disappointment or frustration with finances or career or children. Whatever it is, the health of your marriage will be decisively affected by whether you are able to find ways to do the hard work of grief individually and together, in ways that allow you to cope and even to thrive in the midst of it all.

MYTH 9: THE WAY TO CHOOSE A SPOUSE IS TO LET GOD DO THE CHOOSING FOR YOU

"I was reading books that told me, 'Follow Jesus, pray for your husband, and God will give you the man of your dreams.' So I went looking and praying, and when a boy came along I grabbed him."

There exists a small avalanche of books written by Christian young people for other Christian young people, in which the authors relate the stories of how they found their mates and advise their readers how they can do likewise. These books often express a combination of unbridled enthusiasm for idealized romantic love along with deep skepticism about the contemporary dating scene. The challenge, as the authors of these books see it, is to end up with a perfect fairy-tale romance without in the process having your heart broken by random boyfriends or girlfriends.[2]

A sometimes-proposed solution is that you stop relying on your own judgment and instead wait for God to reveal to you that some particular person is "the one," the perfect partner God has been preparing for you from before the foundation of the world. Until then, your job is to stay free of any emotional entanglement with anyone who is not "the one," to keep your standards high by imagining just how perfect your as-yet-unknown future mate will be, and when God does come through with that special someone, to recognize this person through a kind of spiritual intuition that can be summed up in three words: *You just know*.

This is terrible advice. People learn to love and to be loved not by holding themselves aloof from intimate connection with others but precisely through cultivating intimate relationships of whatever sort. Fantasizing about a perfect future mate does nothing to help you, in all your imperfection, learn to be in relationship with some equally imperfect person who is a good match for you. And imagining that the way to trust God is to disavow any responsibility for—or even conscious awareness of—your own choices is a recipe for disaster.

Of course it is a good idea to trust God. But trusting God and exercising good judgment are not mutually exclusive. You can trust God to be at work in all of your life, all of the time, because that is what God does. Your responsibility is to be thoughtful and engaged, to pay attention to what kind of relationships you are building and who you are building them with, and to depend on God's grace in the midst of whatever mixture of success and failure you may encounter.

MYTH 10: THE WAY TO CHOOSE A SPOUSE IS TO FALL IN LOVE AND THEN MARRY THAT PERSON

"I've heard people say that God wouldn't allow them to love each other if he didn't mean for them to be together."

In the world of idealized romantic love, the mere fact that Cinderella and Prince Charming have fallen in love with each other is sufficient reason for them to get married. In the world of real love and real people, the connection between falling in love and walking down the aisle is never that direct. The mere fact that you love each other is not evidence either that this is God's chosen mate for you or that you would do well to marry this person.

So how do you discern whether a given relationship has the potential to become a stable and satisfying marriage? A few suggestions. First, consider your potential mate's character. Is this person kind? Is he or she honest? Does he or she consider the feelings of others? Can you trust this person to keep his or her word? Can you admire his or her behavior? If the answer to any of these questions is no, then this person is not marriage material. No one should marry anyone who is thoughtless, dishonest, untrustworthy, unkind, or otherwise a person of poor character. Of course we are all works in progress. But when you marry, you put your life in someone else's hands. Be sure you choose someone who is worthy of that trust.

Second, consider how well you get along with this person and the extent to which you share his or her life goals. Do you enjoy one another's company? Do you want similar, or at least compatible, things out of life? Could you develop complementary careers? Can you see yourselves rearing children together? Are your faith commitments compatible? Can you make room for one another's weaknesses or shortcomings? If the answer to any of these questions is no, then marrying one another is probably not a good idea. You don't want to find yourself permanently at odds with your spouse, particularly on matters that you knew were an issue before you married.

Perhaps these points seem obvious. Who would choose to marry a person of poor character? Who would choose to marry someone whose goals they do not share or with whom they cannot get along? Someone who is in love, that's who. It is very easy to fall in love with someone who for one reason or another is not a wise choice, which is why for most of human history "love matches" have been looked upon with skepticism. But we live in a culture in which the refrain, "But I love her (or him)!" is thought to trump any rational objection to a given match, and to be sufficient grounds to marry anyone, regardless of any other consideration. It's not true. Being in love is a fine thing. But just because you love someone doesn't mean you have to marry them.

You may do well to seek out conversation with trusted confidantes about your relationship and your decision-making process. And pay attention to your own feelings and desires too. Do you actually want to marry a given person or not? It is possible to conflate a desire for marriage in general with a desire to marry a particular person. If you have always wanted to be married or you are approaching a time in your life when it seems like you ought to be getting married, it can be easy to suppose that any person who is willing to marry you is the right person for you. It can likewise be easy to fear that if you don't marry this person now, you will never have another chance.

It is true that you cannot know what other opportunities for marriage you may ever have. For this reason, any decision not to marry a particular person is a decision to remain single, at least for now and maybe forever. But while there may have been times and places in which any marriage was better than no marriage, this is not the case in contemporary American society. If you have to make it on your own, you can. This means that you are free to make a good decision about this person and this relationship, and to leave your future in God's hands, where it belongs.[3]

* * * * *

Marriage is a good gift of God. It can be a powerful presence for good in the lives of marital partners, of their children, and of the broader communities they are a part of. You may wish to marry at some point in your life. But you will undoubtedly be single at some point—perhaps more than one point—as well. Fortunately for all of us, both marriage and singleness participate in all the shadows and sorrows of life, and at the same time can be shaped from within by the paradoxical and redeeming love of God.

Chapter Six

Church

AMY PEELER

"DO I HAVE TO GO TO CHURCH?"

"Yes."

It is a rare occasion when I can give such a dogmatic answer. For many student questions, I try to press them out of the black and white and into the gray. I ask them to find the value in the other side of the debate. I invite them to discover the nuance.

Not this question. I even have a proof text from my favorite New Testament book. Hebrews 10:25 says, "Do not neglect the gathering of yourselves together" (translation mine). When students ask if attending church is necessary, I can reply with complete confidence, "Absolutely."

I present my argument for that answer here. If the reader finds it convincing, then another question becomes necessary: How does someone choose *which* church to attend? What factors guide that decision? Are some of those factors more important than others? Is it okay to choose a church because you like things about it?

On the other hand, once students have landed in a particular congregation, they will inevitably discover things they do *not* like. Hence, the final section considers what to do about the aspects you may not like about your church. You can learn a great deal, I've found, by staying in a church that does some things you might disagree with.

It is no secret that college is a challenging time for the development of your ecclesiology, your thoughts about the church. It is a challenging time to develop your thinking about church because at this time your experience of the church undergoes some radical changes. It is often not easy to find a church, and it is even harder to stay committed to it. That being said, the effort is worth the result. The habits developed in these formative years plant seeds for a lifetime of ecclesial harvest.

So, yes, you have to go to church.

I HAVE A GREAT BIBLE STUDY WITH FRIENDS. ISN'T THAT SUFFICIENT?

Some imagine a dorm Bible study might meet the requirements for Hebrews 10:25. In such a setting, students are gathering together with other believers. They are studying God's Word and probably praying for one another. Isn't that what the early church did?

To be fair, I cannot think of a student during my time of teaching who has presented this question to me. At least, not so blatantly. Much more often my students acknowledge that they need to go to church and so ask instead about the best way to decide which one to attend. Maybe, however, this is a question that lurks in the back of their minds, a question they are embarrassed to ask a Bible professor who also works at a church. This seems likely to me because it is a question I frequently asked myself in seminary.

I went to college close to home, so I did not face the culture shock of finding a new church until I moved halfway across the country to attend seminary. My husband and I ended up at a historic church early in our first semester because he was hired as the music director. We had several good months, but soon the pastor moved and the church entered into a time of a pastoral search and interim pastors. The community around the church was also in transition; demographics were changing from one dominant ethnic group to a mix of many different ethnic communities. The interim pastors were great; the congregation was wonderful to us and was seeking to understand its place in a changing world, but it was simply a tough time.

At the same time, some of our neighbors in seminary housing started a small group. Four couples met regularly for meals, prayer, and study. We had deep conversations, we had fun, we were there for each other. I never asked anyone directly, but I wondered it frequently: *If small group felt like church, why did I need to keep going on Sundays?* I would not have been able to articulate a full answer to this question at that point, but here is what I would now say to my twenty-three-year-old self: fellowship with fellow students is a great thing, but it is not a replacement for church.

"Do this in remembrance of me." Some commands of Jesus are not fulfilled in small groups, namely, baptism and the Lord's Supper. Small groups of believers should be telling others about abundant life with God and inviting them to learn more, but if an individual decided to join the group, it would be an odd thing to baptize that friend in the bathtub of the dorm room. It would also be an odd thing for the group of friends to decide to bless bread and wine or juice and practice the Lord's Supper together. These rituals—throughout history—are typically practiced in a church. So, if someone only attends a Bible study, that person would not experience these practices, and Jesus did command them. He told his disciples to baptize those they evangelized in the name of the Father, the Son, and the Holy Spirit (Mt 28:19). At his last meal with his followers, he told them to share the meal in remembrance of him (Lk 22:19), and Paul shows that early congregations were doing just that (1 Cor 11:20-34).

An argument from historical tendency may not be sufficient. Why couldn't a group of friends share the Lord's meal or baptize a new member? There is no proof text from Scripture against such a practice. Another reason against it arises from a second thing a church has that a small group does not.

A view from the outside. The majority of Christians believe that the practices of baptism and Eucharist should be done by someone who has a position of authority that connects all the way back to Jesus. This position of authority could be passed down from the apostles through the process of ordination, or it could lie in the movement of the Spirit of Christ (not that these are mutually exclusive!). Even if it is only the latter, the movement of the Spirit needs to be detected by a *group* of believers over a period of time, not just a small group of friends on a whim.

Churches typically have some built-in accountability, either to an external authority, like a larger group of believers (sister congregations) or a spiritual authority (bishop/diocese). There is someone to act as a check and balance on new ideas or to adjudicate a disagreement. Independent Bible studies and small groups have no such safety net. If there is a debate that turns acrimonious, no one with an external perspective can help bring reconciliation. Even more dangerous, if there is total agreement on an idea that is actually heretical, no one with another body of experience and knowledge can perceive the departure from the truth. That is not to say that churches don't go off the rails, but the propensity for the development of a cult is much greater with a small group of believers.

Students at Christian colleges with regular chapel offerings and even Communion services may assume that their attendance at such events counts as church for them. In such a setting there are good authorities monitoring the orthodoxy of the practices, and clearly some of the practices like Communion are happening. Chapel and Communion shared with other Christians in a college setting are wonderful things that bind that academic community of Christians together, but I daresay that if you asked any college chaplain their opinion on the matter, the reply would be clear. Chapel, even with Communion, cannot replace church. These kinds of settings fail in a very important regard— they do not represent the diversity of the body of Christ.

Many members, one body. It isn't just numbers that protect against heresy; it is the diversity of perspectives within those numbers. This is the third thing a church offers that a small group usually does not—a varied demographic in membership. Typically college students exist in rather homogenous communities. Chiefly, this is true with age. College students rarely interact with children, and unless it is with professors or staff members, they also rarely interact with older adults. Moreover, students at the same college have the same level of education, which often means they have similar ideological commitments, similar

politics, and similar positions on doctrine. If the college is not ethni-
cally diverse, students' diversity may be impoverished in that way
as well.

Many churches do not fare much better in some of those categories,
but it would be an odd church to be made up solely of fairly educated early
twenty-somethings. A church allows space to learn wisdom from others'
life experiences and to learn patience to deal with others' limitations.

It is this enfleshed reality—in all its messiness and beauty—that
makes church church. It is quite easy to watch church online and listen
to great sermons, which is great for the occasion when you cannot get
to church or want more learning. But if this is all someone does, they
are no longer functioning along the model of Christianity itself, which
is incarnational. Being with others in the flesh is a chance to serve
them and depend on them. This is how we practice what Jesus wanted
for his followers when he prayed that we would all be one (Jn 17:22).

Training for the future. It takes time to get to know others well
enough to learn their wisdom or share their burdens, but it is over this
time, the week-in and week-out attendance, that church is offering
another benefit: a habit of life you can carry with you when you
leave college.

College and graduate school provide easy access to an inviting community. A Christian residential setting is one of the best examples: you
walk out your door to a hallway full of like-minded friends. Even if the
educational setting is nonresidential and you do not share the faith of
your fellow students, school is an easy place to meet people, make
friends, and subsequently start a Bible study.

Life outside the educational experience demands more initiative to
form community. You may live in a neighborhood where people often
get to know one another, or you may not. You may connect with people
at work, or they may function out of the belief that mixing work and
friendship is a bad idea. If, however, you have already established the
habit of attending a church outside your educational community, you
are much more likely to continue this habit and go outside your residential or work community. This is another reason why chapel is not

sufficient. When chapel is no longer offered or required, one can embrace their already established habit of attending a local church.

I may not have thought through all of those things when I was in seminary, but my husband and I did keep going to our church even as we continued to enjoy time with our small group. Maybe some weeks it was because the church was my husband's place of employment, but I don't think that was the only thing. That wouldn't explain why *I* went each week. I had some nascent sense that attending was an act of obedience to which I should be faithful. I cannot deny that some weeks it was harder to obey than others, but more often than not I enacted Spirit-facilitated obedience.

Now that I look back with more than a decade of hindsight at our experiences at this church, I can see so many ways that God was blessing our obedience. It was there at church that we learned lessons we've utilized over and over again: how to do a search for an open position, how to have conversations about diversity, how to honor tradition, and also how to try new things. It was also there that we began to discover some of our gifts: for music, for research, for preaching, for leadership. Importantly, we didn't discover these gifts but the precious members of that congregation who recognized things in us that we could not yet see. Neither the seminary classroom nor the living room meetings of the small group could ever offer the same lab for that kind of discovery. We came to realize that church attendance was not only a command we needed to obey but a gift God provided for our edification.

HOW DO I CHOOSE WHICH
CHURCH TO ATTEND?

The ability to be able to ask this question is a blessing. It assumes that one has made a commitment to God's command for congregational gathering. It also assumes the freedom to worship. Many believers across the world do not have this blessing. The question also assumes that you have more than one option, and it assumes the resources to get to more than one option. Not all believers, even in countries with religious freedom, have such blessings. For those who do, this question should first allow us to pause and express gratitude that we can do so. Then, we can steward that blessing well by considering seriously the factors that shape our answer.

I hesitate to present a list of factors, for inevitably I will leave something out that readers deem important, if not vital. The list that follows then is not meant to be comprehensive but only reflects several issues that I and my family, as well as many of my students, have frequently considered as we've worked through the issue of where to attend church.

Regula fidei. At the top of my list stands historic Christian teaching, and historic Christian teaching is founded upon the authority afforded to Scripture. If a church is listening to and preaching the texts of the canon and trying to live in line with Scripture as understood by the majority of the Christian tradition expressed in the historic creeds, the church will be able to hear God's voice and discover God's leading. Clearly, this does not mean that false interpretations could not arise and ugliness would never color the life of the church. Bible-believing churches have problems; such is the pervasive and distorting nature of sin. It is still the case, however, if Scripture is not vibrantly foundational and if core orthodoxy is optional, then such a church will not have access to God's primary means for correction and growth. Neither will the people who attend there.

Live local. A colleague of mine exemplifies this commitment to place. When she and her husband moved to Wheaton, she could walk out her door and see a steeple. "That is where we will go to church." They were committed to living locally and living simply. For them, that meant planting themselves in their neighborhood church. This is, of course, how everyone used to decide where to go to church. You went to the church where you could walk. An embrace of this way of life today returns practitioners to the many benefits of rootedness. You save time and money and environmental impact by not driving. You have more of a chance to know your neighbors as you walk to church, some of whom may also attend the same congregation. You are more likely to get involved in church life because you can get there quickly and easily. This might not be as weighty of an issue as orthodoxy, but in the steps of looking for a congregation, proximity is a great place to begin.

My part of the body of Christ. There may be a church very close to you and it may be orthodox, but it might not be a part of your denomination. Some people have a deep commitment to their denomination and want to remain connected to it even when they move locations. Such a commitment could arise from generations of connection, or, conversely, could display the zeal of a convert. Denominational commitment always has the temptation to turn into idolatry, pride, or factionalism, but this is not inevitable. A healthy allegiance to a denomination affords continued connection to a larger group of believers, and those long-standing relationships create space for continued influence, influence from the denomination and influence upon it. Going to a church of the same denomination also allows the comforts of home; some of the aspects of the church will be the same, and this can make the transition of a move less jarring. At the same time, since each local body of believers establishes its own unique identity, attending a church of the same denomination allows one to see those differences in even sharper relief. This results in gratefulness for what one has known in the past, and appreciation of some new ways of doing things.

During my sabbatical, my family and I had the great opportunity to live in Scotland. It was important for us to stay within our denomination. We wanted that consistency for our children and also wanted to continue to be able to exercise our gifts in ways similar to how we do so at home. The liturgy was largely the same, and that was inviting. We knew what to expect, and we knew what to do during the different moments of the liturgy. Yet upon that backdrop of similarity, the differences were brilliant. Whereas our church is formal, this one was dramatic in its formality and showed to us the beauty and awe of holiness in a new way. Yet its seriousness also made us appreciate the celebratory mode of our worship at home. We both loved home more and were excited to bring new ideas home as we were making connections internationally in our wing of the body of Christ.

For the beauty. For ages humans have articulated their experience of God as goodness, truth, and beauty. In the circles I grew up in, goodness and truth made perfect sense as aspects of God, but beauty was treated as an unnecessary luxury or even as a vice. However, for many throughout the Christian tradition, this has not been the case. Beauty was a way to convey the glory of God to those attending and have those attending rightly worship.

How is the church designed? Does it encourage comfort or awe? Reflection or fellowship? Is there art to contemplate during the service or is the stark simplicity meant to encourage prayerfulness? Being mindful of these kinds of questions allows you to reflect on the sensory settings that allow you to best enter into worship.

Some Christians may not have considered the structure or art of the church, but few have never considered the music. Many churches have joined in—or been dragged into—the worship wars debate, often framed as an opposition between contemporary and traditional music. This is not a new conversation. For centuries Christians have squabbled over the appropriate type of music. Should there be any lyrics other than the psalms? Can the choir sing more than one tune? Should the congregation sing? Should the organ be allowed? So the question of the presence of guitars and drums may be a new medium, but it is not a new issue.

Many different styles can bring glory to God, but there are some aspects to consider. Music should draw one to focus on God and not the musicians or yourself. You may be led to consider God's love for you as an individual or God's creativity as displayed by the talented leaders, but the leading of the music ultimately should be to draw the congregant to the contemplation of God.

Warm welcome. The factors previously discussed may get you into a church, but it will usually take more to keep you there, namely, a sense of welcome, an invitation to participate in the life of the church. Some may wish for a place of retreat and silence when they attend a church, but normally after several visits, most want to be noticed and known. It is a good thing to observe how the church ensures that everyone is greeted, especially those who are new, then take notice of the activities that are offered. Do the clergy do everything, or is the entire congregation encouraged to use its gifts? If so, the church should offer a variety of activities and times for these activities. They should also ideally be open to new ideas when people present new ways to do ministry. The best way to serve together is to provide space to get to know one another. Are there times for fellowship but also the cultivation of genuine community?

As I study the communities of early Christians described in the New Testament, it becomes increasingly clear to me that the foundation for *koinōnia*, for fellowship, was knowledge. They were small enough and honest enough to know what each other needed. They did not do a good job of providing for those needs always and hence needed the exhortations that we can now read, but some of the challenges we face, they did not. It takes time to achieve in many Western cultures today, but true fellowship is possible. If a church provides space for small groups of people to do life together, to share meals, to be in each other's homes, to ask hard questions, to pray, to be vulnerable, then over time and with God's grace, true community is possible. I've seen many beautiful examples in my own experience and in the many testimonies of others.

Faithfulness to God's kingdom leads to another vital but often challenging question: What does this community look like? At base, as I discussed previously, a church should ideally have fellowship between different age groups. One's soul is often fed by the simple joy of a child or the hard-earned wisdom of the aged. One of my greatest gifts is to hear the life story of some of our older parishioners. In a particular time of doubt in my own life, it was the story of an eighty-something year-old friend who shared the miraculous and gracious intervention of God in her life when she had walked away from the faith. Her testimony of God's faithfulness through many decades could never be replaced by even the most ardent faith of one who has only lived to tell the stories of only a few decades.

But for many, age diversity is not enough to reflect the kingdom. They desire the church to manifest Paul's vision of inclusion as articulated in Galatians 3:28. In Christ, different classes, genders, and races find an embrace.

The question of gender is a complicated one. The functioning of women and men in ministry depends heavily on one's interpretation of particular biblical passages and principles. If you are considering a long-term commitment to a church, it is important to ask church leadership about their theology of gender. What can men and women do or not do and why? A church may not align in all respects with your thoughts on these issues (if those thoughts are worked out; for many college students, this is the time to investigate this topic and church may be a great lab to continue to work them out), but an openness to dialogue is vital. You may find yourself in agreement with the church's stance. If you do not, you will have to weigh if the issue is compelling enough for you to find a congregation that does align with your position.

The human gathering in the new heavens and the new earth will comprise every nation and every tribe. For many people, if a local church does not reflect that future diversity, it is not sufficiently in line with God's will. Because of racial segregation in the fabric of history and housing policies, often a person will need to travel to find a congregation that embodies this ideal. Those who discover it come to realize the benefits extend beyond a present reality of the eschatological vision. The diversity of different races brings a diversity of different experiences, different economics, different ways of viewing and living in the world. In a Christian community this allows a refinement and deepening of the understanding of the gospel. What are the gospel's central affirmations, and what are its cultural accretions? If a church is made up of people from the same culture, it is much harder to perceive the difference between the two. Moreover, a community of different races or different classes or both encourages a mutual dependence. Each person as a member of different groups has different gifts to offer and different gifts to receive. Achieving such mutuality is incredibly difficult, but nothing is impossible with God. So these kinds of eschatological communities are possible to discover in the present.

The danger in considering these factors is that finding a church may put us in the position of consumers. Due to the realities of contemporary life, we become the victims of overwhelming choice. We are allowed to choose the church that makes us feel most comfortable and leave that church when it does not meet all our desires (more about that in a moment). But the process does not have to become so degrading.

When we come to 1 Corinthians in my classes and notice that of all the problems Paul tackles in that community he begins with the problem of factionalism, we contemplate how he would feel about the many different denominations in the Christian church. If denominations create inappropriate pride for self and disdain for others resulting in the inability to communicate and partner with those of other camps, he would certainly stand against it. If, however, denominations and their local manifestations in individual churches play to their particular strengths, such as beauty, diversity, exuberance, awe, and service, denominations become less like factions and more like the parts of the body of Christ. If one approaches the multiple choices in this way, we are no longer consumers but pilgrims, seeking to select the place where we can most readily encounter God and most fully serve God's kingdom. Such an approach will help us know how to prioritize the different factors that go into selecting a congregation. We should, ideally, end up in a place that feels like home. That is a recognition of the unique ways God has shaped and formed us, and a recognition that the church is not just an organization but a family. Families demand duty, but on a much deeper level they provide blessing.

REMAINING IN A CHURCH

Families also have tension.

It is one thing to choose a church that aligns with our own particularities. It is another to leave a church because it does not align perfectly. Inevitably, the longer we stay in a congregation, the more we will discover both things we love and things that rub us the wrong way. It is important, then, to consider how to remain and disagree with integrity and also to consider when it might be time to leave. Rather than thinking in the abstract, particular examples flesh out some of the principles at play.

Let's imagine you discover a church. It is close to where you live, it offers several opportunities for outreach in ministries that excite you, the people are extremely welcoming and friendly. The teaching is grounded in Scripture and both challenging and encouraging, so you go back for weeks at a time. It seems like it will be a good fit.

One Sunday, however, you notice in the bulletin that there will be a baptism that day. Your church back home pulled out all the stops for baptism. The person would get to share their testimony, they put on a white robe, and the pastor exuberantly dunked them in the water before everyone. Once a year, your congregation even met at a local lake to get an outdoor experience. It strikes you that in the new church you've been attending, you've never noticed where the baptism font is. *Possibly*, you think to yourself, *it's hidden behind a set of curtains or something and today it will be revealed*.

It never happens. Instead, at the time for baptism a family brings forward a small baby in a frilly white dress, and the pedestal where they normally put flowers has become a largish bowl. The parents speak for the child when asked questions about belief in God, and the pastor barely gets the baby wet as he touches the baby's head with a wet hand three times. In your opinion, the whole process is rather minimal and, more importantly, you are concerned that this baby has no idea what is going on. How can this be a real baptism?

In my humble opinion, such an event would not be a reason to stop attending the church, at least not immediately. Instead, this is an opportunity to discover how faithful Christians approach a vital element of faith differently. Take some time to research your home church's stance on baptism. Why was it important to put someone under water? Why did the person share their testimony first? Then, schedule a visit with someone in your new church to learn about their position on baptism. Why do they baptize infants? What theology is that meant to convey? What do they do to ensure that the baby understands what is going on? You will discover that each has both biblical and historical reasons for what they do. You may decide that believer's baptism (what your home church practiced) is so important to you that you cannot be a part of a church that practices infant baptism, and that would be a principled decision. Conversely, you may realize that you appreciate your new church's practice and have learned something new about this inaugural Christian rite.

I can imagine a similar scenario playing out with the way churches practice the Lord's Supper or spiritual gifts or how they view the end of the world or its beginning. Faithful Christians can approach these topics differently and remain faithful. In the process of discovering a different way, you will begin to learn what is most important to you and why, as well as grow in understanding and appreciation for those who think and practice differently.

Much more difficult may be a situation that you never could have anticipated, such as the revelation of an unfaithful leader or a major doctrinal shift in a denomination. These are not questions of academic imagination but frequently lived realities in the time in which I am writing, and conceivably they will continue to exist. The complexity of such situations makes it impossible for any one-size-fits-all admonition. That being said, it does seem to me that a first reaction should be toward grace and reconciliation. All churches and all denominations are imperfect, and when those imperfections come to the surface, much could be learned by staying in the hard times.

Situations exist, however, when it is appropriate to leave a congregation you have joined. This should not be done lightly and for some inconsequential reason (e.g., urban legends abound about members leaving over a carpet color change). Such a decision demands serious thought, research, prayer, consultation. It will often involve grief as well, but I do see leaving as a viable option. If attending a congregation is continually a frustration in your spiritual life rather than stimulation to growth, it is okay to explore the reasons for the frustration and if any of those reasons are a sign that it is time to move to another place. Leaving can be done amicably, if not painlessly. The grief of that kind of a leaving will be a sign of the love you had for the church and it had for you.

To ask the question of church attendance during college is particularly challenging. Many students at this time move to a new area, many for the first time without their families. Hence, they have all the unsettledness that comes with a location transition along with a new degree of free agency. As their world expands through education, they may feel at dissonance with some of the ways they have grown up, and church is one of those primary locations of growing pains.

In addition to the psychology of it all, the logistics work against students. Many demands vie for their time: classes, activities, friendships. Church attendance may feel hard to fit into that schedule. If a student does get into a good rhythm of attendance, before they know it comes spring break or summer and they are away again, back at home or traveling. It is hard to build up a pattern of consistency.

All that to say, I want students to give themselves grace at this time of life for this area of faithfulness. Partnering with other believers to worship and serve is never easy; doing so during college is even harder. If it takes some time or fits and starts of connection, this is not a bad thing. The only thing to avoid is giving up on the endeavor. God never intended us to walk the journey of the Christian life alone without any connection to corporate worship.

Although I work with Christians and teach the Bible five days a week, I simply cannot imagine my life without church. It keeps me honest in my studies. When I preach, I must think through how the history and the language make a difference in our lives. It exposes me to different questions than those that come from students, questions from children, from retirees, from nonacademics, from those who have grown up outside the evangelical bubble. It shapes the rhythm of my life, marking each week with a fresh reminder of who God is, who I am, and what really matters. It feeds my soul and my spirit.

You will have read that Cyprian the third-century church father said, "He can no longer have God for his Father, who has not the Church for his mother."[1] As someone whose primary research focuses on the gendered dynamics of theological family language, this statement demands an essay (if not a book!) all on its own, but the necessity and blessing of the church is the point I wish to capture here. Calvin does so with beauty in his reflection on this statement. In his *Institutes* he writes,

> But because it is now our intention to discuss the visible church, let us learn even from the simple title "mother" how useful, indeed how necessary, it is that we should know her. For there is no other way to enter into life unless this mother conceive us in her womb, give us birth, nourish us at her breast, and lastly, unless she keep us under her care and guidance until, putting off mortal flesh, we become like the angels [Mt 22:30]. Our weakness does not allow us to be dismissed from her school until we have been pupils all our lives. Furthermore, away from her bosom one cannot hope for any forgiveness of sins or any salvation.[2]

This is a bold statement, but it is completely fitting with Scripture. One cannot do Christianity alone. The church is the gift God has provided for all God's people to survive and to thrive until we dwell in God's presence forever.

Maybe by this point in my life, I've arrived at a better answer to the initial question, "Do I have to go to church?" Yes, I would say, you *get* to go to church, and it is incredibly worth the effort to find the right one, now and at every stage of life.

Chapter Seven

Wealth and Power

JAMES G. HUFF JR.

DAVID ZAC NIRINGIYE STOOD COMFORTABLY, with a slight grin, in front of the crowded classroom of sixty mostly first- and second-year college students. Earlier that week a group expressed to me their excitement about getting to hear from a Ugandan pastor and theologian. Nearing the end of the semester, some students had started to ask the questions that always seem to emerge then: How are we to live now in light of all that we have learned together? I thought it especially timely that Dr. Niringiye agreed to join our discussions and ponderings. In fact, I was secretly hoping that he might conclusively address some of the challenging questions the students were asking me!

For most of his adult life, Bishop Zac, as many affectionately call him, served as assistant bishop of the diocese of Kampala for the Church of Uganda. He was one of several guest lecturers who visited our course "Poverty, Justice, and Transformation" that fall semester. His relaxed posture and warm smile put the class at ease. What came out his mouth next startled more than a few.

"The problem with the world today is not poverty," he stated calmly. Bishop Zac, ever the master rhetorician, then paused for effect. He continued, "It is greed!" His voice boomed as his arms widened and spread out beyond the width of his shoulders as if to indicate that we all were being incorporated into his claim. He lingered again, waiting for the silence to generate a mix of discomfort and anticipation. A playful grin slowly returned to his face. Most of the students listened with rapt attention. Some looked a little uneasy.

It was not the first time we had heard something like this. Earlier we had spent one class responding to a short reading by philosopher Nicholas Wolterstorff. In the chapter, Wolterstorff considers the early church fathers' teachings on poverty and wealth. The admonitions of Basil the Great provoked lively discussion:

> Will not one be called a thief who steals the garment of one already clothed, and is one deserving of any other title who will not clothe the naked if he is able to do so? That bread which you keep, belongs to the hungry; that coat which you preserve in your wardrobe, to the naked; that gold which you have hidden in the ground, to the needy. Wherefore, as often as you were able to help others, and refused, so often did you do them wrong.[1]

Wait a minute, some wondered, *how could the wealth of the rich belong to the poor? How could my hard-earned income and stuff possibly* belong *to someone in need? Does this mean I'm supposed to give whatever I have to people in need that I encounter in everyday life?* At the time I was content to let the questions linger. But Bishop Zac was reviving them. As the lecture continued, he started to sound a whole lot like Basil.

Students are often surprised by the questions they start to ask themselves and others as we study global poverty and development. Many sign up for the course anticipating that we will focus on determining effective forms of poverty alleviation. And we do consider such questions. Eventually. But these and related questions—which I like to call the "what are we supposed to do?" questions—are problematic, mostly because they leave other equally important inquiries unasked.

In *Reconciling All Things*, Emmanuel Katongole and Chris Rice observe that the problem with the "what do we do?" question is that it never interrogates the "we."[2] The query generally assumes that the only people in need of change are those who are presumably poor, vulnerable, and powerless. It does not ask us to prayerfully consider our own complicity in the problems we encounter in the world. Moreover, it reflects assumptions we often maintain about ourselves, and especially about our ability to use our wealth and power to generate change in the lives of other people. We tend to "think of ourselves as an innocent solution delivering help to places of human need."[3] I suspect that this is partly why the words of an ancient church father and a Ugandan pastor provoked the responses they did: their claims interrogated the "we."

ACKNOWLEDGING THE COMMUNITY
FROM WHICH WE ASK

Before exploring some of the specific questions that my students and I consider, it is important to clarify the larger context our questions emerge from. Who is asking and responding to questions about wealth and power matter, as do the dynamic patterns of culture, religion, ethnicity, and socioeconomic status that comprise the fabric of our learning community.

The one constant in the conversations we have is me. As a forty-something, married, white man who is a homeowner in a mostly white, suburban community, I possess considerable stocks of wealth and power. I was born into and have frequently lived and worked in environments that have granted me a very privileged status. And while I have worked hard to achieve some of the social and material rewards that matter to the culture in which I grew up, I recognize that I belong to social groups that are especially privileged in US society. Very few are the occasions in my life when people have identified me as someone who should be treated differently because I am a white man. Rare are the times when I have wondered if who I am or how others perceive me might complicate my efforts to belong or to participate. Rather, for most of my life I have been treated favorably by others simply because my social categories are treated accordingly by the dominant society.

The setting where we interact is also a learning community composed of people who bring their diverse backgrounds and life experiences to bear on the questions of wealth and power. Yet it is also a place where certain voices and perspectives remain predominant and privileged. The college where I work is mostly a white community, for example. So, for a large number of students—namely, those who grew up in white, upper-middle class, evangelical households—it can feel like home from day one. For the small but growing number of students of color, participating in college life often requires considerable courage and perseverance because it may not readily feel like home. It is not uncommon for students of color to express feeling out of place, and for some the college experience is often a conflicted one. It is a season of life when meaningful learning occurs and when vocational aspirations are affirmed. But it can also be a time when some students wonder, *How much of who I am will I have to give up to succeed and belong here?*[4]

Why name all of this? Mostly, I want to acknowledge that the reflections I offer here are partial. Not in the sense that they are half-baked, but they are limited, and they should be considered prudently by readers as such. In pursuing practical wisdom on ethical matters related to wealth and power, we should rely on the counsel of many. This means intentionally seeking guidance from diverse voices. My own perspectives on wealth and power have been transformed by colleagues and students who have experienced systems of power and privilege in ways that contrast considerably with my own. We need to be very clear about the crisscrossing and sometimes contradictory patterns of difference and privilege that make up our learning community. The questions that we ask, or don't think to ask, emerge from this very dynamic context.

WHAT DO WE MEAN BY WEALTH AND POWER?

Of the two concepts, wealth seems a bit more straightforward to define. A common misunderstanding is that wealth is synonymous with having lots of money. To be wealthy is to be rich in a sense. But such richness takes multiple forms. This becomes especially apparent when we consider the various ways that human beings across space and time have attached value to the stuff, relationships, knowledge, and places that matter to them. One helpful definition posits that wealth is any attribute of a person that contributes to the flow of valued goods and services in a group or society.[5]

Note what this broad definition does and does not imply. It connotes that wealth is not just the material stuff we value. The power that material forms of wealth have in our lives demands special attention to be sure. But there are many other attributes that a person can possess besides money, land, smartphones, or investment accounts that are valuable to them. No doubt you have heard someone described as being "rich in relationships." The phrase acknowledges the significant value of friendships and social connections. Wealth, then, is also a relational attribute. It is also *embodied*, meaning that wealth refers to things like bodily health, knowledge, and practical know-how.

Seeing wealth in such a multidimensional way reminds us of how we human beings attach value to all sorts of things. It seems that our proclivity to *treasure* is an innate capacity. We are very capable of investing our whole lives into treasuring; in fact, and we do so in very ordinary ways, regardless of how much cash is in the bank. Jesus, a very astute observer of the human condition, once remarked, "The place where your treasure is, is the place you will most want to be, and end up being" (Mt 6:21 *The Message*). The critical point is this: when we talk about wealth of any kind, we are talking as much about our treasures as we are about our treasuring.

I think power is a bit more challenging to define. Social scientists regularly debate its definition. At its core, though, power is fundamentally about influence. To borrow a simple definition, power is a "far-reaching process of influence."[6] We can readily see how this works in everyday settings. Take, for example, what occurs when a professor asks students to engage in small group discussion. The professor's request is usually straightforward and, most of the time, students comply. But how they actually behave is far from uniform. How the actual practice of small group discussion unfolds is the product of a dynamic process enacted by the teacher and students together. What occurs in real time is a process of power exercises—efforts by the students and professor to try to make something happen. Some exercises are obvious and directly observable. But others are only discernible through careful observation over time. For example, research demonstrates that shared norms concerning how women and men should participate in discussions influence classroom interactions. Generally speaking, the relatively few male students in my class tend to hold the mic a lot longer than their female counterparts. What happens in class is also influenced by culturally prescribed gender roles and by shared ideas about the relative value of women and men's contributions to public discussion.

A lot more could be said about power, but this simple example demonstrates the ordinariness and ubiquity of power. Our relationships are suffused with it. We often think of power in entirely negative terms. It does not take long to think of a powerful person who exercises influence in destructive ways. But as Andy Crouch has observed, the good and right use of power is also fundamental for the flourishing of all people and of creation.[7] This means that we need to be sober about the dangers of destructive power even as we discover how power can be exercised for creativity and for life.

WHO WE LISTEN TO PROMPTS NEW QUESTIONS

Over the years I've noted that the questions students ask during office hours or over a cafeteria meal are rarely about wealth and power, at least not in any direct or explicit way. It could be that relatively few would identify themselves as wealthy or powerful in the first place. In part this suggests something about our communities: one of the privileges that comes with being wealthy and powerful is not having to think about our status all that much. So, getting to questions about wealth and power is something that emerges over time. We usually meander our way to them via other inquiry pathways. How the questions evolve as we wander seems to have something to do with who we listen to and learn from along the way.

As noted, some students begin by asking about how to best help those in need. Accordingly, they inquire about which forms of outreach or development are the most effective. What are the best strategies to resolve poverty? What are the proven approaches that empower people to work for good change in their lives and communities? Many more wonder about which efforts to support. How are we to know if an organization is actually making a difference? How are we to decide which one to support? These are all very important questions to consider, and we do begin to address them. Nevertheless, such questions reflect deeper ideas and assumptions that require more reflection and attention.

One of those ideas concerns how we tend to think about our relationship to valued attributes and possessions, however little or great the quantity. Take discussions in some Christian circles about the proper stewardship of money. Such talk, argues Richard Foster, views money, "almost without exception . . . as completely neutral and depersonalized."[8] He adds that many of us think accordingly: "God has given us money to use, to administer, to put into service. . . . And so the emphasis is always placed upon the best use, the proper stewardship, of the resources God has entrusted to us." Such an assumption helps to explain the questions students ordinarily pose: they are questions we often ask about how *we* should best allocate *our* wealth and exercise *our* influence. Foster argues that we not stop there with the questioning: "What all this talk about stewardship fails to see is that money is not just a neutral medium of exchange but a 'power' with a life of its own. . . . As long as we think of money in impersonal terms alone, no moral problems exist outside the proper use of it."[9]

What happens along the way, then, that prompts us to ask new questions about wealth and power, and specifically about our relationship to them? The process seems to unfold in one of two ways. The first occurs among many of the first- and second-year students enrolled in Poverty, Justice, and Transformation. In the course, we read the stories of ordinary people residing in villages and towns in Nigeria, El Salvador, and India, who are living in the midst of considerable economic, political, and social change. Their narratives confront the "single stories," to quote Chimamanda Ngozi Adichie, many of us have about poverty in the so-called Majority World.[10] They are stories of protagonists who actively confront economic deprivation, chronic injustice, and forced displacement, but they are also portrayals of the resilience, resourcefulness, creativity, *and* power of vulnerable people.

Listening to their stories greatly complicates our understanding of poverty and wealth. For instance, such stories help us understand how poverty is fundamentally relational. We see that poverty involves the rich and poor alike, and we recognize it is as a process that binds them both together in "mutual dependence and struggle."[11] Such stories help us to become aware of the connections between our lives and the lives of distant others. For example, in the course we trace out the links between the consumption of highly valued goods and services (e.g., smartphones) and the labor of young and often highly exploited miners of minerals in the Democratic Republic of Congo. Such learning is not an exercise that aims to induce guilt. Rather, it simply illuminates how our lives are enmeshed with the lives of vulnerable others—again, the rich and poor bound together in "mutual dependence and struggle." This directs us to not only reconsider our ideas about the causes and consequences of poverty but also prompts new insights and questions about our wealth and power.

For some students it provokes a rather straightforward realization, *Wait a minute, I am wealthy!* True, there may be more than a few cash-poor (and indebted) students running around our colleges. But the very fact that we attend, work at, and study in a university places us squarely in the category of the world's wealthy. If we are dishonest about our wealth, then it is difficult to take seriously Jesus' radical critique of it. So, being honest about our wealth is an important first step.

Others raise more complicated questions. Most common among these are critical reflections related to their ordinary habits of consumption. Some begin to recognize the pervasive reality of detachment in their own lives as consumers. Ruth Valerio, in her book *Just Living: Faith and Community in the Age of Consumerism*, observes that it is no accident we tend to view our wealth in a very decontextualized manner. On this point she refers to the theologian Vincent Miller: "Our countless acts of consumption and evaluation of commodities large and small train us daily to value things *out of their contexts*."[12] This detachment from context is built into the very fabric of our modern global economies—and it signals how we are generally ignorant of the people or the environments (God's creation) from which our wealth is created and produced.

Critical recognition of our cultural default as detached consumers prompts some students to ask, How can I learn more about where my stuff comes from? How can I ensure that what I purchase is made by someone in good working conditions? How can I make sure that it was produced in ways that are also good for God's creation? What am I to do when I recognize that my wealth has come at the expense of others? These are very complicated questions, of course. In fact, I avoid offering formulaic responses to them. But making a habit of ordinarily and regularly asking them can help us all to develop what Valerio calls an "ethical instinct: an underlying understanding of how our consumer system works and the main issues to look out for."[13] These new, everyday habits of inquiry are small acts to be sure. But they are an important step in learning to work quietly against the problematic forces of detachment that are part and parcel of the economies and societies we inhabit. They also orient us to think critically about the far-reaching influence and cumulative power of our consumption habits.

"GETTING PROXIMATE"

Let's consider another way by which students begin to ask new questions. It is a somewhat exceptional process of discovery. I say exceptional because they are questions asked by students who spend an extended period of time living and working in the communities they read about in my Poverty, Justice, and Transformation course. The program I work in prepares and sends approximately twenty-five students each year to participate in a six-month internship where they work in a low-income or sociopolitically marginalized community located in Latin America, Asia, Africa, or the Middle East. Their learning is fundamentally experiential, fully immersive, and deeply relational.

These students spend their hours and days in the company of a host family and with neighbors who teach them how to live, interact, communicate, and worship in ways that are meaningful to the members of their host community. In their work settings each student learns from local professionals—including doctors, social workers, psychologists, lawyers, pastors, and entrepreneurs, to name a few—who invest their lives into addressing the problems of poverty and powerlessness in their neighborhoods. As you can imagine, such an extended period of learning from and with unfamiliar neighbors generates all sorts of questions. And by "getting proximate," to borrow a phrase from author Bryan Stevenson, students become especially aware of the dynamics of power and wealth, both their own and others'.[14] How so?

First, as guests they learn that their well-being is fundamentally dependent on the generosity, creativity, work, and hospitality of people who they once simply identified as "the poor." They recognize how they are no longer *in charge* of their lives. Rather, they experience firsthand how their living is sustained and made possible by the influence, resources, know-how, and friendships of their Guatemalan or Zambian host families and neighbors. One student, for example, recounted a surprising experience he had in the church he attended in an urban, squatter community where he resided in Manila, Philippines. During one Sunday morning service, he realized that he was used as an illustration in a teaching on the parable of the Good Samaritan. In the sermon, the student was the foreigner in need, who was lying in the ditch on the side of the road. He had never considered himself accordingly. As the sermon continued, the pastor reminded the listeners that the well-being of the vulnerable foreigner-neighbor, who they frequently encountered in the narrow alleyways of their slum community, would be assured by the time, energy, and resources they shared with him.

At the same time, getting proximate exposes students' own power and wealth, which they acknowledge as taken-for-granted realities. One student in our program recognized the considerable power of her citizenship and ethnic status as she spent six months working alongside internally displaced and refugee families living near the Thai-Burmese border. She could come and go with relative ease while her neighbors' movements were intensely controlled and under constant surveillance. Another recognized how little it cost her to purchase medicines to treat the frequent stomach illnesses that she experienced as she adjusted to life (and food!) in a new community. The meds were also needed by neighbors to treat similar ailments, but the costs were often too great. This meant that treatment had to be frequently delayed and the illness consequently remained. What seemed to be a minor illness, that was in fact easily treatable, was a burden to bear, and one that sapped the energy and strength of many neighbors in her host community.

The insights and questions that emerge from such person-to-person encounters go beyond wondering about how to become an ethical consumer. It is upon returning home, which for most is somewhere in the United States, that the questions start to pour in. They are different questions that they ask as they begin their final semester as college students: How am I to continue to accompany, listen to, and learn from those who ordinarily confront poverty and powerlessness in my home community? And how exactly I am to do this, especially since the neighborhood where I reside is a place where I rarely have the chance to interact with neighbors who face such realities? And what about in my church, where the only opportunity I have to meet new neighbors is through the occasional outreach event? How exactly do I build enduring relationships that bridge the divides of class and power that are a part of the neighborhood where I reside and are often reproduced in the church where I worship? How do I continue the practice of being a good guest, who is ordinarily dependent on the hospitality and generosity of others? How do I continue the learning journey of becoming a good host who regularly shares my home, friendship, and table with strangers in my neighborhood? You will note that these are not questions that direct us to devise a strategy, technique, or program that allows us to remain unchanged as we try to "change the world." They are questions, in fact, that call for our own ongoing conversion along the way.

CONFRONTING THE POWERS: SOME VOWS TO LIVE BY

There is no shortage of good Christian writing on how to practically address the questions we have regarding wealth. Notably, there are considerably fewer such readings on power. An excellent resource that carefully considers both is Richard Foster's book *The Challenge of the Disciplined Life: Christian Reflections on Money, Sex, and Power*. My copy of his book is by now a dog-eared, well-worn, and thoroughly highlighted copy. I appreciate Foster's use of very down-to-earth language. He also maintains a winsome tone even as he tackles challenging ethical questions. The practical advice he offers regarding how we might bring the good news of Jesus' kingdom to bear upon our wealth and power is especially encouraging and, in the end, doable. To be clear, it does not answer many of the questions outlined in the preceding sections of this chapter. But I think it can direct us to become the kind of people who make a habit of searching out answers to these questions in the communities where we reside and among the people we interact with there.

His advice is helpful in large part because it is very sober about the *powers* of wealth and power. He reminds us of how Jesus warns his followers and listeners—over and over again—about the dark side of wealth. Why the repetitious and radical critique? Because Jesus is matter-of-fact about the god-like powers that animate wealth and money in particular: "For Christ money is an idolatry we must be converted *from* in order to be converted *to* him. . . . And in point of fact, money has many of the characteristics of deity. It gives us security, can induce guilt, gives us freedom, gives us power and seems to be omnipresent."[15] Similarly, the New Testament has a lot to say about power, and especially about the pervasive workings of powers both visible and invisible. Foster observes, "Power profoundly impacts our interpersonal relationships, our social relationships, and our relationship with God. Nothing touches us more profoundly for good or for ill than power."[16]

Perhaps the first practical point of departure for us all, then, is to reacquaint ourselves with how plainly Jesus and the rest of the biblical narrative speak about the spiritual reality of wealth and power. They are not merely neutral instruments or resources that only require our good stewardship. Such thinking is simply too naive about the spiritual powers that seek to distort them. Foster, like Bishop Zac, reminds us how capable we are of sustaining quiet and pervasive greed for wealth and power. This is a truth that makes plain the great power that both can have over our hearts and our lives.

Thankfully, his insights do not stop with a detailing of the destructive capacities of wealth and power. Both can and should be used for God's purposes and aims. Wealth, in other words, has a light side and power can be creative. The relationships we cherish, the good health we experience, the know-how we develop, the beautiful environments we inhabit, and even the money in our bank are all necessary for living. Of course, we must learn to put money in its proper place alongside all of these other forms of wealth. This might simply involve learning how to recognize that the money we make is fundamentally dependent on so many other wealths that are not the result of our own efforts: "Everything that God created is good, very good. . . . Most wonderful of all is how so much of what comes is not the result of our own doing but a gift, unearned and unearnable."[17] Power too can be a creative force for great good in the world. Power that proceeds from God "creates restored relationships and gives the gift of wholeness to all."[18] I am reminded of one student who spent his six-month internship collecting and recording stories of reconciliation among people who survived the Rwandan genocide in 1994. They were narratives of forgiveness and of reconciliation between the perpetrators of brutal violence and the victims whose loved ones were murdered. They are stories that give witness to the power of the resurrection.

So how are we to become the sort of people who ordinarily relate to and use wealth and power to bring goodness, restoration, beauty, and wholeness to our lives, to our relationships, and to the world? Foster invites us to make two vows that will direct our treasuring and in-fluence toward the good of others and for the wholeness of God's cre-ation. The first vow is simplicity, which according to Foster is neither an option "for the dedicated few" nor one that we "take or leave de-pending on our personal preference."[19] Rather, it is a commitment that we all as Jesus-followers are to embody and live out. The vow has many practical facets. Two are worth mentioning here because they are the ones that my students noticed in the lives of families and neighbors they lived with during their six-month internships. First, they learned that simplicity means being available. They witnessed this as they were hosted by people who were not enslaved to "the compulsion of ever bigger or ever better," and who consequently, had "the time to respond to human need."[20] Second, it also means giving joyfully and generously: "we give of ourselves, and we give the product of our life's work."[21]

The second vow is service. Like simplicity, it is a multidimensional commitment. It is the "ministry of the towel" that Jesus practices when he shows his disciples how power is to be exercised.[22] To live this way means a life of everyday obedience to God. Making a vow to serve accordingly means that we disable our inclination to problem solve in a knee-jerk fashion or based solely on our own capacities, strengths, and resources. Instead, we stop and listen. Foster reminds us the Latin root of *obedience* means "to listen."[23] We first listen to God's promptings and to the unfamiliar voices of those we seek to serve. Finally, the vow of service also means compassion, which "puts us in touch with all people."[24] Most of all, compassion calls for a willingness to be especially with and among those who suffer. According to Henri Nouwen, the development of a disposition of withness means that we understand that "compassion asks to go where it hurts, to enter into the places of pain, to share in brokenness, fear, confusion, anguish."[25]

Note what such vows do and do not imply. They imply a kind of settled disposition that is fundamentally about love of God and of neighbor. They are about living a life of joyful abandonment to God and of generous care for others. They are vows, then, that enable us to practically confront and contradict the destructive forces of wealth and power that are so often at work in the contexts where we live and work. Note too that they are not commitments that we live out only after we accumulate a certain quantity of valued goods, or only when we have extra time on our hands, or when we one day have a platform. They are vows that we learn to routinely practice in the here and now. Again, my students have frequently commented on how their hosts in Peru or Thailand have carefully calibrated their own resources according to the needs of others. Generosity was a built-in quality, so to speak, of how they ordinarily went about using their wealth and power. They were daily habits of simplicity and service that made possible the experience of "generosity, magnanimity, and shalom" by all who were present.[26] And by treasuring things that endure and that are eternal, their hosts gave practical witness to that "marvelous reality, God's kingdom now."[27]

Chapter Eight

Suffering

DAVID LAUBER

MY SON WAS FOURTEEN WHEN HE WAS DIAGNOSED with acute lymphoblastic leukemia. My wife and I received the news in the middle of the night, and I signed consent to treat forms at 3:07 a.m. There is no good time to be told that your child has cancer, but the darkness of night increases its weight. Some might describe a scenario like this as surreal. I remember thinking at the time that this is as real as life gets. Suffering, especially suffering that appears to come out of nowhere, demands our focused attention. It clarifies many things, even as it clouds others. Whether clarity or confusion, nothing stays the same.

Suffering raises many questions and elicits various responses. When people found out that our son had cancer, they asked us, "Do the doctors know what caused it?" "Was it because of his diet?" "Is it genetic?" They wanted an explanation, otherwise the randomness of it was too unsettling. Perhaps they were worried that something like this could happen to their own child and they needed to know how to prevent it. Other people assured us of their concern and care, "We're praying for a miracle!" "This is horrible. I feel so sad." These remarks were genuine and well-meaning. But I really did not need to be told that this was horrible, and I did not have the energy to comfort others in their own distress.

I believe God answers prayers and might choose to act miraculously, but at the time I did not want to hear that a miracle was the only way forward. I needed to trust the expertise of the medical staff and the effectiveness of the treatment protocol. Still others attempted to re-assure us: "It will be exciting to see how this fits into God's plan for him." "He will have an amazing testimony!" The resilience and cheerful endurance my son has shown tells me that his character will be refined and strengthened. I look forward to hearing him talk about his three-year cancer treatment as a pivotal but past episode of his adolescence. However, it is difficult for me to see how this must be a necessary component of God's detailed plan for his life.

While these questions and comments were not entirely helpful to me, I recognize that people genuinely cared and wanted to say some-thing encouraging. When we face suffering, whether our own or that of others, we seek answers. We want explanations. We want to look on the bright side of things. We desperately want control. In sum, we want a textbook answer to our personal trials and questions. I understand where these questions and comments come from. I asked these and other questions myself. I wanted to believe the confident words of ex-planation. Yet this was insufficient. I needed more. And over time it became clear to me that I needed to rely on God's grace.

I have taught an introductory course in theology for a number of years, and I know the range of textbook answers to the questions raised by suffering. Every time I teach this course the topic of suffering and evil stimulates urgent class discussions. Every student has expe-rienced some type of suffering and is searching for ways to respond. I have grown accustomed to discussing evil and suffering as an essential theological topic. I think I have heard just about every possible question, and my teaching experience has made me proficient in giving what I consider to be intelligent, faithful, and wise answers and counsel. But the existential force of my son's precarious medical situation com-pelled me to ask critical theological, pastoral, and personal questions in a new way.

Upon receiving my son's diagnosis, I felt deep within my mind and heart something that later I discovered was stated plainly by C. S. Lewis in *A Grief Observed*: "You never know how much you really believe anything until its truth or falsehood becomes a matter of life and death to you."[1] I'm sure I believed the things I taught my students, but the life-and-death reality of a sick child cut through my doctrinal competence and the self-assured assessment of my own faith.

I am well aware of the fact that people endure numerous types of suffering, including incurable cancer, violence, oppression, injustice, hatred, abuse, mental illness, chronic physical illness and pain, sudden death, and the long list goes on. Much of this suffering is more severe and devastating than treatable childhood leukemia. But as they say, "write what you know." Today, the story of my son and family is the one I know best. I will offer what I know, not as a template into which all instances of suffering must or can fit. Rather, I offer these reflections as one account of God's gracious presence in the midst of concrete suffering.

TEXTBOOK ANSWERS

Frequently the question "How can a good God allow horrendous evil and suffering?" is referred to as the "problem of evil." When we phrase it this way, we seem to be suggesting that evil is a question that can be answered, a puzzle that can be solved, or a phenomenon that can be explained. The difficulty with approaching the reality of evil and suffering this way is that it implies that we can solve it through intellectual analysis and argument. This could leave the personal reality of suffering untouched and unresolved. I think the attempt to provide an analytic solution to a general account of suffering is futile. Suffering is always concrete and particular. It takes place in specific contexts, with particular people and circumstances.

Sometimes an explanation of suffering points to retribution. People suffer because they deserve it. God is just and God justly punishes people for their sin. Note that this is the account of suffering that is given by Job's friends, and he will have none of it (Job 42:7), and God will have none of it. Jesus rejects this explanation in John 9:3, in response to his disciples' question about whose sin caused a man to be born blind—his own sin or the sins of his parents. This type of explanation adds insult to injury. Not only do people suffer, but they are guilty for their suffering. And it makes it difficult to have compassion for those who suffer. Should I really have compassion for someone who is suffering if their suffering is the result of their own sin and the consequence of God's judgment? It seems that compassion and the attempt to alleviate suffering would be ruled out, lest we get in the way of God's judgment. Furthermore, it calls into question the obvious inequitable distribution of suffering. For example, do we really want to say that one group of people is more guilty than another group because the suffering they experience is more severe and devastating as a result of a hurricane? Is it collective guilt, or is it simply a matter of vast differences in infrastructure and resources?

Another approach is to claim that suffering is somehow good for us. Suffering builds character, helps us grow, tests our faith, teaches us something important. Yes, this can be the case, but this is not to say that suffering always achieves this end. I agree with friends who have encouraged me that my son will develop strength of character by enduring the months of chemotherapy treatment for his leukemia. I also trust that I will learn many things and will be changed in significant ways as I witness the suffering, treatment, and healing of my son. But it is inconceivable to me that somehow God gave my son cancer to teach me things I need to learn. I want to grieve and condemn this dreadful disease, even as I pray that God will work graciously in and through it.

The view that suffering is necessary in order to build character gives too much meaning to suffering. It says that suffering in and of itself leads to these positive outcomes. This explanation overlooks situations in which suffering simply results in destruction, devastation, and despair. Moreover, it underestimates the significance of God's grace. It is, after all, God's grace, which works through these instances of suffering, that leads to a positive outcome. It is not something that is inevitable because of a structural element of the suffering itself.

In my judgment, both of these views are inadequate and unhelpful. They say too much. By rationally explaining the reality of suffering and by proposing the necessity of evil and suffering, all of a sudden evil and suffering are not only explained, but they are also explained away. Suffering is no longer suffering and evil is no longer evil. Evil and suffering are now good because they fit somehow into God's overarching plan.

Scripture and the good news of the gospel of Jesus, I suggest, do not directly answer the question of *why* evil and suffering exist. Rather, Scripture and the gospel of Jesus bear witness to God's presence and action within a world marked by evil and suffering. Christian faith upholds God's loving, comforting, and redeeming presence and action. Scripture bears witness to the reality and the promise that God's loving and gracious goodness is powerful to bring good out of suffering—to raise up those who are devastated by the pain of the world—to establish life in the midst of a world in bondage to death. It is one thing to say that God can and does bring good out of suffering and a completely other thing to say that suffering in and of itself is meaningful, good, and necessary.

THE MYSTERY OF EVIL AND SUFFERING

Often Christians think that in order to be faithful they need to affirm that everything that happens in the world, from the greatest blessing to the most painful tragedy, is the direct result of God's action and is perfectly in accordance with his active will. Think of the common remark "Everything happens for a reason." In this instance something that sounds theologically significant—if God is powerful and sovereign, then he must directly cause everything that happens—is, on close examination, mistaken. Although an appeal to God's providence and lordship is important, we must take care that we do not claim to know more than we are allowed to know.

My suggestion is that Scripture presents us with a view of God's relationship to suffering in which we are to avoid two extremes. The first extreme identifies suffering with the direct will and action of God. In this view God is the immediate and direct cause of everything that happens in the world, including suffering. This, however, is fatalism. It makes God the author of evil and suffering, and this is not what

Christian faith means by God's providence. The second extreme accounts for the presence of suffering by maintaining that God is incapable of doing anything about it. In this view, God is a distant observer and spectator of our world. This, however, is deism and also is not what Christian faith affirms as God's providence.

The Christian doctrine of providence invites us to occupy a space within these two extremes, a space Todd Billings describes as the "mysterious middle."[2] God's providence refers not to God as the only cause of everything that happens in the world. God's providence refers to God's lordship over the world. God mysteriously allows or permits things to happen even though God does not directly cause everything to happen. God sustains, governs, and directs the world to his intended end, but God does not directly cause every event in the world. God is good and powerful. God holds the world in his hands. God is Lord over the world, and there is nothing that slips through his fingers. Billings quotes N. T. Wright in describing the power and permission of God in relation to suffering and evil: "the scriptural narrative tells us 'in no uncertain terms that God will contain evil, that he will restrain it, that he will prevent it from doing its worst, and that he will even on occasion use the malice of human beings to further his own strange purposes.' Yet while we affirm this, if we ask the question of why 'God will not simply abolish evil from his world,' we 'are not given an answer.'"[3]

LORD, HEAR OUR PRAYER

Sometimes faithful Christians are convinced that in order to display their strong faith and confidence in God they must always be happy. After all, doesn't Paul insist that we are to "Rejoice in the Lord always. I will say it again: Rejoice!" (Phil 4:4)? While it is certainly true that we can experience the joy of the Lord even in the midst of painful situations, we cannot underestimate the power of sadness and grief. Furthermore, we cannot neglect the stark words of sorrow, dejection, desolation, and even despair and depression that we find within the pages of the Bible, where, for example, we read,

I am weary with my moaning;
  every night I flood my bed with tears;
I drench my couch with my weeping.
  My eyes waste away because of grief. (Ps 6:6-7 ESV)

In recent years there has been increasing interest in the Christian practice of lament. Many people are returning to Scripture, in particular the psalms of lament, in order to find ways to express their grief and pain in the face of their own suffering or the suffering that surrounds us in society and the world. This is a significant development. Suffering often leaves us speechless, and Scripture gives us the language we need. Lament enables us to express rightly our pain and frustration before God.

Lament protects us from two common temptations. The first temptation is the result of something we could call uncritical optimism or addiction to success. We are commonly optimistic, at least in public. We desperately want to be seen as successful, independent, self-sufficient, fulfilled, and happy. We are strong and self-reliant people. This temptation leads many people to posture before others—to project an aura of control and command of a situation. To express one's pain publicly is seen as a sign of weakness. And weakness and dependence are not acceptable in a society infatuated with success.

There is a popular approach to suffering within some Christian circles that risks resembling this unreflective optimism and addiction to success. Sometimes people attempt to exhibit their faith and trust in God by saying something like "don't waste your suffering." The intention of this phrase has some merit. Don't allow your suffering to keep you from experiencing the gracious presence of God. Don't allow your suffering to define you and overwhelm you to the point of despair. However, if we are not careful, this slogan can quickly turn into a triumphalistic and self-satisfied promotion of one's own strength, one's own faith. It resembles the common description of cancer patients as warriors who are battling and will defeat their disease. Or if they die, it will be at the end of a valiant struggle. It could even lead someone to conclude that God caused them to suffer because he knew that they were strong enough to handle it, that they would bear witness to God in the way they managed this trial. Here we twist suffering and a theology of the cross into a self-preoccupied theology of glory.[4]

Should Christians hope that they will bear witness to God's power and grace in the way they walk through suffering and pain? Absolutely. But this certainly is not something that we can judge for ourselves. We can only receive this judgment and evaluation from others, and even if we are admired for our faithfulness and witness, we should never seek this in a self-serving way, as if we have another achievement that we can bring to God expecting a commendation. We need to be careful of focusing on our own faith; instead, we need to focus on God, who is the object of our faith. Our faith may indeed be firm, but it might also be weak and wavering. In any case the God in whom we place our faith is strong and trustworthy.

Another temptation we face arises out of aspects of a therapeutic culture. We are sometimes encouraged to vent our frustrations, express our complaints, and seek someone or something to blame for our situation and unhappiness. I've even been in situations when there was a competition to see who could tell the most depressing and painful story. "So you think you are broken and have suffered? Let me tell you my story. It's much worse!" This is emotional purging, but it is not shaped by hope and trust in God. This might provide us some psychological relief for a time and enable us to cope, but it will not lead to the peace and redemption promised and enacted by God. If the first temptation prevents us from expressing honestly grief and sorrow, this temptation keeps us from demonstrating contentment and hopefulness in the midst of suffering. Lament shows us how to do both.

Biblical lament demonstrates that we can express our pain before God. We can come to him with a full range of emotions—grief, anger, outrage, and fear. God can take it. God is not offended by the deep pain we feel as we encounter difficult and uncertain situations. We do not need to put on the false face of strength. At the same time, biblical lament arises out of faith. To lament before God is to acknowledge him and trust him. Biblical lament is not merely venting our frustration in hopes of gaining some kind of release. To lament faithfully before God is to come before God honestly as we have been laid bare and cut to the core because of life's difficulties, pain, and sorrow. We come before God openly and honestly because we trust that God hears us. We trust that God will respond to us. We trust that God will comfort and save us.

Scholars have identified typical components of lament psalms. We can see these components in Psalm 13, one of the clearest examples of a psalm of lament. To lament before God is not to shout in the dark. It is a shout that is directed to God. The psalm begins with an *address to God*, "How long, O LORD?" (ESV). After addressing God, the psalmist provides a specific *expression of lament*,

> Will you forget me forever?
>> How long will you hide your face from me?
> How long must I take counsel in my soul
>> and have sorrow in my heart all the day?
> How long shall my enemy be exalted over me? (vv. 1-2)

The particular expression of lament is followed by a specific petition:

> Consider and answer me, O LORD my God;
>> light up my eyes, lest I sleep the sleep of death,
> lest my enemy say, 'I have prevailed over him,'
>> lest my foes rejoice because I am shaken. (vv. 3-4)

This shows us that we are invited to bring before God specific requests and petitions that arise from the uniqueness of our own situations. The series of honest and urgent questions and requests leads to an *exclamation or confession of trust in God*:

> But I have trusted in your steadfast love;
>> my heart shall rejoice in your salvation. (v. 5)

Notice that the psalmist does not appeal to God's power and control, which might lead him to accept his plight dispassionately. The psalmist places his confidence in God's character and his promise. He trusts

God's steadfast love and anticipates God's mighty act of salvation. Finally, the psalmist expresses a *vow of gratitude and praise*:

> I will sing to the LORD,
>   because he has dealt bountifully with me. (v. 6)

The words of lament in Psalm 13 express the unique individual experience of David, and they seek God's attention and action to alter his own situation. These words can guide us as we cry out to God from the midst of our own sorrow. Lament also shapes the way we can encounter and respond to the suffering and pain of others. We not only lament and cry out for ourselves, but we also lament and protest before God as we encounter the pain and suffering of others.

In June 2015, Otis Moss III, pastor of Trinity United Church of Christ in Chicago, and his father, Otis Moss Jr., preached a tag-team sermon titled "Prophetic Grief." This was not a sermon on the general theme of grief, the abstract topic of evil. This sermon and its call to grieve prophetically was just a few days after a white gunman entered a black church in Charleston, South Carolina. He killed nine people and wounded three as they were gathered for an evening prayer meeting. This sermon arose from a particular situation of hatred and violence, suffering and death. It gave powerful voice to true Christian lament and live-giving Christian hope. The preachers contrasted "prophetic grief" with "pathetic grief" and "sympathetic grief." They described pathetic grief as "angry, mad, vicious, and bitter—always blaming others." And they described sympathetic grief as instances in which we "pass out sympathy without necessarily entering into the other person's tragic moment." In prophetic grief, by contrast, we "stand within the other's wounds, and hurt, and blood, and tears, and sorrow—so deeply, that it becomes our own."[5] The Mosses pointed to African American Christians, whose history is marked by agony, as a profound witness to this type of grief. The agony is real and named, but as people of faith and hope, they will not allow the agony to define and imprison them. Through God's strength, these Christians were and are able to follow the way of righteousness and live through agony to the "blessed assurance of everlasting affirmation." This form of grief is prophetic because it bears witness to the power of God's righteousness and the strength of love to produce healing and redemption in the midst of pain and sorrow. "Love is stronger than hate. God's grace is stronger than our grief. And God's power is greater than our pain."

To lament is to live between remembrance and anticipation, between memory and hope. We remember God's character, his past saving actions, and his promises to us. And on the basis of this remembrance, we anticipate God's redeeming action in the future. It is this remembering and anticipation that enables us to bear faithful witness to God's grace, love, and power in the midst of dark and difficult situations.

THE TEARS OF JESUS

We can learn much about how God is present in our concrete situations of suffering by exploring Jesus' encounter with Martha and Mary as they grieve the death of Lazarus. Both Martha and Mary meet Jesus with the exclamation, "Lord, if you had been here, my brother would not have died" (Jn 11:21, 32 ESV). This is a statement that many people make. "Had you been here" could also be phrased more strongly as a question or accusation, "Where were you?"

This statement "Lord, had you been here . . ." and the implicit question "Why weren't you here?" lead us to seek explanations for the suffering and evil we witness and experience firsthand. Jesus hears the word of both complaint and trust from Martha and Mary. They trust that Jesus could have done something had he been there. And they complain, lament, or protest his absence. "If you had been here my brother would not have died." Jesus hears our pain and our questions. He hears the fervent question of the psalmist—"How long, O LORD?"

Jesus not only hears our pain and our questions, but he also responds to our pain and questions with compassion. He is the revelation and presence of the one whose "compassion is over all that he has made" (Ps 145:9 NRSV), "the Father of compassion and the God of all comfort" (2 Cor 1:3 NIV). After encountering the identical statements of Mary and Martha, we see Jesus responding to their grief and mourning. "When Jesus saw her weeping, and the Jews who came with her also weeping, he was greatly disturbed in spirit and deeply moved" (Jn 11:33 NRSV). When Jesus sees the sadness and grief of those who are mourning the death of Lazarus, he too becomes sad and grieves. He not only grieves the death of his friend Lazarus, but he is also "greatly disturbed in spirit." This means that he is angry, indignant, even outraged. Some commentators suggest that Jesus is outraged by what he considers to be the lack of faith and trust by those who are mourning Lazarus's death. The plain reading, it seems to me, is that Jesus is responding to the source of the grief and mourning. He is angered by suffering and death. He sees the world in all of its brokenness, distortion, corruption, and pain. He sees people who are bound by the tight hold of evil, pain, and suffering, and he wants to deliver them.

We then read in John 11:35 that "Jesus began to weep." We all know that this is the shortest verse in the Bible. The King James Version of this verse is the familiar two-word statement, "Jesus wept." It is not only the go-to verse for middle school Sunday school students who need to come to church with a verse memorized, but it is also one of the most profound verses in the Bible. It is worth pondering. How does Jesus, the incarnate Lord, act in the midst of a world marked by horrific suffering, evil, and pain? Jesus weeps. This is not a tear on demand in order to posture before an audience—to project an image of compassion and empathy. It is genuine. Jesus' tears well up from his heart.

We can see the significance of Jesus' weeping as we join it to Paul's exhortation in Romans 12:15 to "weep with those who weep" and Jesus' own words in Matthew 5:4, "Blessed are those who mourn, for they will be comforted." Jesus' weeping at the tomb of Lazarus shows us that he mourns with those who mourn; he weeps with those who weep. Jesus not only shows solidarity with those who suffer and grieve, but as God's comforting presence, Jesus also fulfills the promise that those who mourn will indeed be comforted.

LIVING WITH SUFFERING: HOPE, PATIENCE, AND PRAYER

A number of years ago I heard Gary Haugen, the founder and president of International Justice Mission (IJM), speak about the difficulties of humanitarian work. After outlining a number of challenges he and his organization face every day, he pointed to Paul's exhortation in Romans 12 as a truth of Scripture that sustains him. In Romans 12:12 Paul encourages the believers in Rome to "rejoice in hope, be patient in suffering, and persevere in prayer" (NRSV). I left that evening impressed by the way Haugen appealed to Paul in order to face situations of horrific suffering with compassion and resolve, and to celebrate the positive results of IJM's faithful efforts. For example, the statistics on sex trafficking are staggering. The problem appears to be too overwhelming to change. Yet we can celebrate the particular work done to rescue particular people from the clutches of the sex trade. Will IJM eradicate sex trafficking completely? No. But, has IJM freed particular girls and women from brothels throughout the world? Yes! This work is fueled by a commitment to justice and it is sustained by the hope of the gospel, patient and persistent endurance, and constant prayer.

I have come to see Romans 12:12 as my personal prayer for my theology students. I do want them to be able to articulate the coherence of Christian beliefs as I teach essential aspects of Christian doctrine. But my main goal for them is that they grow in wisdom, that they will develop into mature Christians whose lives after Wheaton will be marked by hope, patience, and prayer. This has everything to do with living faithfully and wisely in suffering and affliction.

Rejoice in hope. To rejoice in hope is not to dismiss or underestimate the reality of pain and suffering. It is to name the suffering for what it is, but to not be overcome by it. Hope does not ignore the gravity of suffering and pain. Christian hope is thoroughly realistic. We can unflinchingly describe the potentially overwhelming realities of suffering and pain, but because of God's power and transformative work, we are not overcome by suffering.

One challenge we face in striving to be hopeful people in the midst of suffering is to be hopeful without being triumphalistic. This takes some spiritual dexterity. We should seek to be hopeful without being naively optimistic, even as we should seek to be realistic without being overly fearful and despairing.

Gratitude is also related to hope. As we rejoice in hope, we give thanks for God's presence and gifts. This too involves spiritual dexterity. We need to learn how to be grateful without forgetting the pain and suffering of others. We need to be drawn out of our inward and isolating focus on our own situation so we can see people around us. In my own experience of accompanying my son to the children's hospital and oncology clinic, I am confronted directly with the challenge of giving thanks for my son's consistently improved medical condition even as I see children and families who are enduring great pain and heartache. We must be able to give thanks with humility while we pray and grieve with others, as we hope with and for them.

Be patient in suffering. To be patient in suffering or adversity is to exhibit long-suffering endurance. Patience is not passive resignation to one's circumstances. Patience is active and persistent. To be long-suffering is a demonstration of strength in the face of obstacles. Because we have hope we can bear patiently suffering, affliction, and adversity. Again, patience is not stoic resignation or indifference. To be patient is to trust in God. Patience is active waiting. It is to acknowledge one's need and dependence, and humbly receive and rely on the help of God and others.

Persevere in prayer. Paul frequently calls his people to prayer—to "persevere in prayer" (Rom 12:12 NRSV) or "pray without ceasing" (1 Thess 5:17 NRSV) or "do not be anxious about anything, but in every situation, by prayer and petition, with thanksgiving, present your requests to God" (Phil 4:6). These calls to pray at all times and for all things are akin to Jesus' invitation to consider the lilies of the field and not be anxious, and do not worry about tomorrow (Mt 6:28, 34). To persevere in prayer is to recognize that we live before God, constantly in his presence. It is to trust the one to whom we pray. It is to know

God as our heavenly Father, who watches over us, sustains us, cares for us, and guides us. The one who rules over this world and over our individual lives is not a generic all-powerful, all-knowing, and domineering god. The God who rules over the world is our Father, who provides for us, who makes himself known to us in the tender and humble love of his Son, and who draws us to himself through the sure and gentle work of the Holy Spirit. We are to persevere in prayer to this God. We are to cast all of our cares on this trustworthy God, who is with us and for us.

WEEPING MAY LINGER FOR THE NIGHT, BUT JOY COMES WITH THE MORNING

I replay the night of March 30, 2017, over and over in my mind. During that dark night of a cancer diagnosis and the days that immediately followed, there were glimpses of God's grace and intimations of real hope. As we were driving to the children's hospital in Chicago from our Wheaton home, the word *believe* came to my wife's mind again and again. This summons to believe and trust our trustworthy God calmed and protected her then and it continues to sustain her now through the ups and downs of accompanying our son on his journey toward complete remission. The tears of an ER doctor showed us humane compassion in the sterile and institutional environment of a large urban hospital. The gentle yet firm words of assurance from the oncology fellow who delivered the news to us gave us a way so see through the fog of shock and grief. "We know what it is. We know how to treat it. Our plan is to cure him." The concern shown by my daughter and son for their younger brother revealed a reservoir of love that was present in our family and continues to nourish their consistent care for him.

As a father of a seriously sick child, it could be easy for me to slip into self-preoccupation by focusing on my own anxiety and grief. Yet I understood early on that although this is indeed difficult for me and for my wife, it is my son who is ill. This is obvious, I know. But it is often overlooked as we attend to our own feelings in witnessing the suffering of others. He is the one who has endured dozens of chemotherapy treatments, fatigue, nausea, fevers, bouts of pancreatitis, many nights in the hospital, missed days of school, and the list goes on. I remarked then and have continued to tell people since that he has shown great resilience and quiet and calm confidence. He trusts God, and he trusts his doctors. Early on, as people expressed grave concern and worry about him, he said to me. "I won't worry unless my doctors are worried. I trust most those who know the most." His faith is sure, but not simplistic. He grieves the losses to his childhood, and in lament he has wondered what might have been—"I wish it had been mono." Through it all he has displayed patience, hopefulness, and trust. I need to honor the way he has approached his disease and treatment, and learn from him even as I seek to support and encourage him.

I write these things not to highlight the strength and faith of my son (or myself and my family) as if it is uncommon. I know many people in difficult situations who bear faithful witness to the grace of God. I write these things as a testimony to the light of Christ in the midst of darkness.

On the occasions when I pray the compline prayer before going to sleep, I pray for my son and those close to me. I also pray for people unknown to me. I am grateful that God, whose love is steadfast and grace is sure, receives my prayers. I have come to see today that the first words I spoke to my wife that March night—"Remember, we are not alone"—were a gift of God's grace. And I give humble thanks to God for welcoming the prayers of those who unknowingly prayed for me that night.

> Keep watch, dear Lord, with those who work, or watch, or weep this night, and give your angels charge over those who sleep. Tend the sick, Lord Christ; give rest to the weary, bless the dying, soothe the suffering, pity the afflicted, shield the joyous; and all for your love's sake. Amen. (Book of Common Prayer, "Order for Compline")

Chapter Nine

Doubt

KEITH L. JOHNSON

A STUDENT RECENTLY VISITED MY OFFICE to discuss some concerns she was having about her Christian faith. As we talked, it became clear that she had several important questions about God and salvation that she could not answer with confidence. Although she desired to have faith in Christ, she did not feel sure about what she believed. She worried that her doubt was a sign of sinful rebellion against God, but she simply could not resolve it on her own.

Our discussion reminded me of the story of the father who sought out Jesus in Mark 9:14-29. The story is dramatic because the father needed a miracle. His son had a spiritual affliction that often left him on the ground, seized up, and foaming at the mouth. The terror could strike at any moment. Once, his son had been standing next to the fire and then fell into it, causing terrible scars. Another time he was cast into the water and nearly drowned. The father worried about his son constantly, and he rarely let him stray from his sight. No doctor had been able to help. Maybe Jesus could do something.

He brought his son out to meet Jesus, but when they arrived they found only a few of his disciples because Jesus had gone to a nearby mountain. But the father thought that perhaps these disciples could help. At the father's request, they tried to cast out the evil spirit. They failed just like everyone else. Then the situation started to grow chaotic. Some scribes began arguing with the disciples about the technicalities of the Jewish law. A crowd began to gather, with voices rising and elbows jostling. The father became anxious, and his son became agitated. The father likely began to worry that this journey to Jesus had been a mistake.

Then suddenly a shout arose from the crowd, "Jesus is coming!" The man's heart must have leaped into his throat as the people parted to let Jesus through. "What are you arguing about with them?" Jesus asked his disciples.

With courage born of desperation, the father spoke up. "Teacher, I brought you my son; he has a spirit that makes him unable to speak; and whenever it seizes him, it dashes him down; and he foams and grinds his teeth and becomes rigid; and I asked your disciples to cast it out, but they could not do so."[1]

Jesus looked at the boy, and then he looked at his disciples and the agitated crowd. "You faithless generation, how much longer must I be among you? How much longer must I put up with you? Bring him to me." The man led his son forward to meet Jesus, but at that precise moment the spirit who possessed him stuck the boy down. He fell to the ground and began to roll in the dirt. The father tried to hold him to keep him from harm.

"How long has this been happening to him?" Jesus asked. The father told him it had been taking place since childhood. And then, clutching his son in his arms, he added: "But if you are able to do anything, have pity on us and help us."

As I imagine the story, I suspect that Jesus probably let out a sound that seemed close to a chuckle. "If you are able!—All things can be done for the one who believes."

Immediately the father cried out, "I believe; help my unbelief!" The words probably came out before the father could think about them, but they reflected his heart. He did believe, or at least he *hoped* to believe. Why else would he have come to Jesus? But of course he also had doubts. No one had been able to help his son. Why would Jesus be any different? He did not want to get his hopes up. And who was this Jesus anyway? Where did he come from? The father had so many questions, and they kept him from being certain. Yet his son needed a miracle, and he was willing to trust this man Jesus in the midst of his doubts.

The crowd began to tighten around them. Then Jesus said, "You spirit that keeps this boy from speaking and hearing, I command you, come out of him, and never enter him again!" The boy cried out, convulsed, and then grew still. "Is he dead?" people in the crowd asked in whispers. But Jesus took the boy's hand and lifted him up until he stood. He was healed.

As I read and discussed this story from Mark 9 to my student, it showed her that she was not alone in her doubts. In fact, the father stands in the place of every believer, because the entire Christian life occurs within the dynamic of faith and doubt. Christians have faith in Jesus Christ—that is what makes them Christian. But they also are called to *understand* the things they say they believe. To this end the church traditionally has drawn a distinction between faith and fideism, which is the "reliance upon faith alone, accompanied by a consequence disparagement of reason."[2] But applying the standard of reason to the claims of the faith sometimes means that questions are raised for which answers are not immediately available. There are limits to human knowledge, because "we walk by faith, not by sight" (2 Cor 5:7) and "see in a mirror, dimly" (1 Cor 13:12). These unanswered questions leave room for doubt to arise. Do the claims of faith make sense? Are they really true? How can anyone ever be sure?

I told my student that doubt is not the opposite of faith. Doubt often is simply the form faith takes as Christians venture beyond the limits of their comprehension. It is not necessarily a sign of disobedience. Rather, doubt often results directly from a believer's obedience to the command to "take every thought captive" to Christ (2 Cor 10:5). This does not mean that doubt should be taken lightly or embraced. Christians always should be moving from doubt toward confidence. But that journey can be long and difficult, perhaps even lasting a lifetime. And it is a journey that requires help from Christ. The father's words belong to every Christian: "I believe; help my unbelief!"

WHAT IS DOUBT?

Several different Greek words are translated into English Bibles as "doubt." The first is *distazō*, which means "to hesitate." Jesus uses this word when Peter begins to sink while walking on the water. Even though Peter was brave enough to get out of the boat, the strong winds and waves made him hesitate in fear. Jesus responds by immediately pulling Peter out the water. "You of little faith," he said, "why did you doubt?" (Mt 14:31). Later, Matthew uses the same word to describe the disciples after Christ's resurrection. As they gather on the mountain to receive the Great Commission from Jesus, something inside of them causes them to hold back from a full commitment: "they worshiped him; but some doubted" (Mt 28:17).

Luke uses the Greek word *dialogizomai* in a similar way to describe the disciples' doubt after Jesus' resurrection. This verb is related to the English word for dialogue, and it is used to describe an internal conflict that arises as an argument is considered from multiple angles. Again, the term communicates hesitation and inaction. The risen Jesus applies it to his disciples after they are struck with terror and think they might be seeing a ghost. "Why are you frightened, and why do doubts arise in your hearts?" (Lk 24:38).

A different word shows up when Jesus instructs his disciples about the importance of faith. After causing the fruitless fig tree to wither at his command, Jesus tells the disciples that they will be able to perform similar miracles if they "have faith and do not doubt" (Mt 21:21). The Greek word here is *diakrinō*, which means "to be at odds with." The same root is used to talk about the separation of one thing from another. It depicts people who are indecisive because they are internally divided and unable to make up their minds. James uses this word while describing how believers should present their requests to God. "Ask in faith," he says, "never doubting, for the one who doubts is like a wave of the sea, driven and tossed by the wind; for the doubter, being double-minded and unstable in every way, must not expect to receive anything from the Lord" (Jas 1:6-7). Later in his letter James uses another word for "double-minded," the Greek word *dipsychos*. This word depicts someone who lives in such internal tension that they cannot move forward with confidence.

Taken together, these terms provide a picture of what a doubter looks like according to the Bible. Doubt is not equivalent to unbelief or a lack of faith. Rather, a doubter possesses faith but hesitates to act on it. Something causes them to hold themselves back from God. They are indecisive because their minds are divided. Questions have arisen that they do not know how to resolve. As they consider the possibilities, they exist in a state of suspended animation, unable to move toward Jesus but not rejecting him either. They believe in Christ but lack confidence in this belief. They are at odds with themselves, and so when they hear Christ's call to follow, they remain stuck in place.

ARE THERE DIFFERENT KINDS OF DOUBT?

Some doubts are intellectual and others are relational. It is important to distinguish between these different kinds of doubt and their causes.

Intellectual doubt tends to arise as Christians seek to understand what they believe. The desire to understand one's faith is an act of obedience because Jesus instructed his followers to love God with their minds as well as their heart, soul, and strength (Mt 22:37). Part of loving God with one's mind is understanding the content of one's faith. To this end Paul prayed that believers would have "the riches of assured understanding" that should come with faith in Christ (Col 2:2). Yet seeking to understand one's faith requires courage because it requires believers to examine and test what they believe. This process can prompt new and difficult questions.

To illustrate the challenge involved, think of a mechanic who wants to understand the inner workings of a car. To gain this understanding, he will need to do more than simply look at the engine. He will have to take the engine apart, examine each part closely, understand how they relate to one another, and then put the engine back together. The entire process of disassembling and reassembling the car will provide the mechanic with a deeper and more accurate understanding of its operation. Christians who seek to understand their faith work in much the same way. To know what they believe, they have to examine the various claims they affirm, understand their implications, and discern how they relate. The problem is that this process often raises new and difficult questions that a believer cannot immediately answer. Think again about the mechanic. He might disassemble an engine only to realize that he does not know what a particular part does or how it works in relation to the others. "I wonder what this thing is for," he says. As he goes about his work, the mechanic might receive conflicting information from the people around him. "In my model of car, that part goes here," one person might say. But another person might respond, "No, that part fits over here." The mechanic eventually may realize that he does not know how to put the engine back together. At some point, doubt arises: "Will I ever be able to make this car run again?"

Christians often end up in a similar position. As they seek to understand their faith, problems arise that they may have never considered before. Or perhaps they are exposed to challenges raised by the questions of others. Out of the desire to give an accounting for what they believe (1 Pet 3:15), they might examine their faith only to realize that they do not have a good account to offer. Along the way, they might receive conflicting advice about how the various doctrines of the faith hold together. Doubt can show up in any of these scenarios as the Christian either begins to lack confidence in the claims of the faith or in their ability to understand them.

Intellectual doubts also can arise because a believer has other convictions that stand in tension with their faith. For example, a person might say, "I doubt that Jesus Christ rose from the dead" because she is certain that dead people cannot rise from the grave. Or she might say, "I cannot believe that God is good" because she is convinced that God has directly caused her to suffer. In these cases resolving the doubt involves examining the competing claims, assessing their accuracy, and then either abandoning or revising one or more of the claims. Other doubts stem from the lack of firm conviction. This kind of doubt often arises from a perceived absence of evidence for Christian claims. A person might say, "There is no proof that Jesus Christ rose from the dead." Or they might say, "I have no basis from which I can say that God is good." Resolving these doubts requires assembling enough evidence to help the believer assent to the claims of the faith. In these cases the challenge often centers on the criteria used to weigh the evidence. A person who doubts the claims of the Christian faith usually presupposes an undoubted set of criteria by which their faith should be assessed. He might say, "I will not believe that Jesus rose from the dead until I can prove it historically." This argument presupposes that resurrections are the kind of thing that can be verified through historical investigation. But is this criterion itself valid? This means that in addition to assembling enough evidence to warrant assent, the believer also has to examine the way the judgment is being made.[3]

Along with intellectual doubt, many Christians fall into relational doubt. This kind of doubt stems from a lack of confidence in God's character or the sense that God cannot be trusted. Such feelings often show up after an experience of harm or suffering. "If God is really good, then why has God allowed this evil to occur?" Christians also can experience relational doubt in more subtle ways. As they go about their daily lives, Christians sometimes begin to wonder if their faith in God makes any difference. Or perhaps they look at their flawed lives and wonder if they can ever measure up to who God calls them to be. Martin Luther talked about this kind this kind of doubt as a form of spiritual tribulation marked by the internal conflict between the human conscience and the gospel of Christ.[4] As believers recognize the depth of their sin, they sometimes doubt that God really loves them or can use them in ministry. They may start to view Christ as a harsh judge instead of a merciful Savior, and they doubt whether Christ's promises of grace and mercy can be believed.

John Calvin argued that this kind of thinking has its roots in the contradiction between the way Scripture presents Christ and the believer's experience of the Christian life. Questions arise because Christian's "circumstances are all in opposition to the promises of God. He promises us immortality; yet we are surrounded by mortality and corruption. He declares that he accounts us just; yet we are covered with sins."[5] Doubt often fills the gap between a believer's expectations of the Christian life and its reality, and this doubt is rooted in questions about God's character. The church often exacerbates rather than mitigates this kind of doubt because Christians regularly fail to live up to their calling. While examples of faithful believers abound, the history of the church also is full of unfaithful Christians who foster division, commit sinful deeds, and turn people away from Christ. All of these realties feed the presence of doubt. A believer might ask, "If the church does not measure up to God's promises, and if my life does not measure up either, then does God really keep his word?"

IS IT SINFUL FOR A CHRISTIAN TO DOUBT?

The Bible does not encourage believers to embrace doubt, but it does not always condemn doubt as sinful. Instead, doubt is depicted as a product of the frailty that comes with being a finite and fallen human being.

Those who argue that doubt is always sinful tend to assume that the claims of the Christian faith must be held with absolute certainty. They insist that doubt is a sign of unfaithfulness, a distrustful act of turning away from God. But this approach stems from a distorted notion of faith. Christians traditionally have not required absolute certainty on every point of doctrine because such certainty is categorically impossible for finite creatures. After all, humans are not God, and they do not know God as God knows himself. God knows himself directly and immediately, but humans know God indirectly through the mediation of the created realties God uses in his self-revelation.[6] The knowledge of God humans have through faith is real and true, but it is merely creaturely knowledge. Even as humans know God through created things, God's divine nature remains invisible to direct human perception (Rom 1:20). This explains why human knowledge of God is by faith rather than sight (2 Cor 5:7). Believers will not see God directly until their final redemption when they will see God "as he is" (1 Jn 3:2). As Paul puts it, "For now we see in a mirror, dimly, but then we will see face to face. Now I know only in part; then I will know fully" (1 Cor 13:12). Until this fuller knowledge occurs, many things of God will remain beyond human comprehension.

The fact that life with God involves an ongoing encounter with mystery explains why Hebrews defines faith as "the assurance of things hoped for, the conviction of things not seen" (Heb 11:1). Having an assurance of something or holding a conviction about it is different from possessing an absolute rational certainty. Christians can be certain about what they believe, but they must remember that this is the certainty of *faith*. Faith involves trust in the promises and character of the God whose divine being transcends all creaturely capacities and thus has not yet been seen directly. Again, as Paul puts it, "O the depth of the riches and wisdom and knowledge of God! How unsearchable are his judgments and how inscrutable his ways!" (Rom 11:33-34).

BUT WHAT ABOUT THE WARNING GIVEN IN JAMES?

James issues strong remarks about doubt at the beginning of his letter:

> If any of you is lacking in wisdom, ask God, who gives to all generously and ungrudgingly, and it will be given to you. But ask in faith, never doubting, for the one who doubts is like a wave of the sea, driven and tossed by the wind; for the doubter, being double-minded and unstable in every way, must not expect to receive anything from the Lord. (Jas 1:5-8)

The key to interpreting these remarks is to understand that James's primary purpose in this passage is to point to God's generosity. He is saying that because God does not hold back from helping his people, no one should hold themselves back from God. A person in need should ask God for help with confidence that they will receive this help. A doubter in this instance is someone who does not ask God for help because they assume God will not give it. James's point is that a person who does not ask for help will not receive it.

These insights about God's generosity provide context for James's comments on doubt. His goal is not to condemn all doubters everywhere.

Rather, he wants to encourage people to present their needs to God—including their need to overcome doubt. If someone lacks knowledge about something, they should ask God for help. This is good news because every Christian will be in this position at some point when it comes to their understanding of the faith.

DID THOMAS SIN WHEN HE DOUBTED THE RESURRECTION?

The passage about Thomas's doubt occurs at the end of the Gospel of John, and it has to be interpreted in light of the purpose for which John wrote it. The story begins after the resurrection, when the risen Jesus meets his disciples by appearing to them in the midst of a locked room. He shows them his pierced hands and side and then gives them the Spirit as he had promised (Jn 20:19-23). Thomas was not present for this initial meeting. After hearing the disciples' report, he wanted more evidence. "Unless I see the mark of the nails in his hands, and put my finger in the mark of the nails and my hand in his side, I will not believe" (Jn 20:25). A week later, Jesus once again appears in the middle of the room. Thomas is present this time, and Jesus says to him: "Put your finger here and see my hands. Reach out your hand and put it in my side. Do not doubt but believe" (Jn 20:27).

The key to interpreting this passage is to watch how Jesus relates to Thomas. Jesus does not condemn Thomas for his doubt or scold him for wanting more evidence. Instead, Jesus simply presents his wounds to Thomas and calls him to believe. And Thomas immediately responds with faith: "My Lord and my God!" (Jn 20:28). The way Jesus approaches Thomas—and the way Thomas responds to Jesus—reveals John's purpose for the passage. John's goal is not to portray Thomas as a sinful doubter whose example is to be avoided at all costs. Rather, John presents Thomas as a *role model* for Christians. The reader is called to come to faith in Jesus in the same way that Thomas came to faith in Jesus. Indeed, this is precisely how Jesus himself sees Thomas: "Have you believed because you have seen me? Blessed are those who have not seen and yet have come to believe" (Jn 20:29). The point is that John's readers should follow Thomas's example by also believing in Jesus.

It is never wrong to seek evidence about the things of God. In fact, the Bible praises people who desire evidence, just as the Jews in Berea are praised for responding to the gospel by searching the Scriptures "to see whether these things were so" (Acts 17:11). Seeking further knowledge about God—even if this search raises difficult questions— is precisely what someone who has faith in Jesus should do.

CAN DOUBT LEAD TO SIN?

Doubt crosses into sin when a person stops trying to address it. Thomas doubted the resurrection, but he did not sin as he did so. His doubt arose because of his limited knowledge and his inability to make sense of what he heard. He had sincere questions that prevented him from affirming that Christ was alive, and he wanted more information to answer these questions. This is the key: Thomas sought to address the causes of his doubt. He was willing to learn, and he embraced the truth immediately after Jesus appeared to him. Pilate was different. When he met Jesus, he doubted the truth of Jesus' words but did not seek further information. His question "What is truth?" was more of a statement than an inquiry (Jn 18:38). Pilate embraced doubt as an ongoing posture of life, and this posture enabled him to defer respon- sibility for making a decision about Jesus. His example serves as a warning: doubt that becomes an end in itself strays into sin.

A helpful way to assess doubt is to ask about its trajectory. Where is one's doubt leading to? Is the person with doubt seeking answers to their questions? Are they willing to listen to other people and learn new information? Or have they embraced doubt as a permanent state of being? Are they using the presence of doubt to defer making a judgment or to justify certain beliefs and behaviors? Is the mind of the doubter open or closed? A posture of doubt often is viewed as a mark of open-mindedness. Instead of embracing the unreflective faith of the simple, doubters are seen as intelligent, authentic, and even heroic. As Charles Taylor observes, they often view their willingness to doubt as an act of liberation from the "earlier, confining horizons, or illusions, or limitations of knowledge."[7] But this static posture of doubt can be as closed-minded as any other belief.

The Pharisees display this kind of closed-mindedness during their encounters with Jesus. To be fair, both their prior experience and their theological commitments legitimately prompted them to doubt that Jesus was the Messiah. Many others before Jesus had falsely claimed the title of Messiah, and Jesus did not fit their expectation for how the promised Messiah would live and act. But instead of seeking information and listening to Jesus with an open mind, they decided in advance that he was a false teacher. Because they were confident that they possessed the truth, they approached Jesus with arrogance instead of humility. They asked Jesus questions, but these questions were designed to embarrass and entrap him rather than learn from him (Mt 22:15). These activities stand in stark contrast to a faithful and open-minded approach to doubt. Having an open mind does not require a person to place their doubt aside, avoid asking questions, or stop thinking for themselves. But it does require a willingness to listen, learn new things, and change one's mind when necessary.

Doubt also strays into sin when it becomes an obsession. A Christian might be so focused on their doubts that they spend all of their time thinking about themselves rather than God. Instead of focusing on God's promises, they concentrate on their uncertainties and remain unable to move forward in their faith. The mirror image of this problem occurs when the doubter becomes indifferent or apathetic about God and their faith. The extreme form of this is agnosticism, which is a suspension of belief in God that endures permanently. More often, a person might believe in God but question whether God cares about them or makes a difference within the world. They might affirm key doctrines but wonder if these commitments actually matter. Often this mindset is based on a perceived lack of closeness to God or a person's sense that they do not feel God's presence in their lives. Doubt of this sort often leads to the sin of sloth because it can be used to justify not seeking to grow in the faith. Questions remain unaddressed, problems stay unsolved, and a person shows no concern to move beyond their present state. Doubt also can manifest itself in more subtle ways. For example, a believer might be confident in their convictions but live in a manner that betrays these convictions. This kind of doubt shows up whenever a Christian believes in God but makes decisions as if God is not really a factor.

Doubt also moves into sin when it becomes unbelief. To be clear: a person who doubts does not fall simply into unbelief, and unbelief cannot occur by accident due to a misunderstanding. Rather, unbelief reflects an intentional decision to reject God. Some people reject God on moral grounds in response to the existence of evil and suffering. Others simply deny God's existence and embrace atheism. In these cases, doubt has turned into a sinful certainty that marks a willful turning away from God.

CAN GOD USE DOUBT FOR GOOD?

Doubt should not be excluded from Paul's claim that "all things work together for good for those who love God" (Rom 8:28). There are at least three ways that God can produce good out of the experience of doubt.

First, God can use doubt to propel Christians into a deeper understanding of their faith. Doubt often arises because Christians find that their prior beliefs no longer make sense. This discovery can happen suddenly or gradually over time. An experience of suffering might prompt hard questions about God's character. A person might enter a new stage of life and find that the faith of their youth no longer suffices, or they might realize they have an incomplete grasp of what they thought they believed. A person might receive objections to the faith they cannot answer, or they might encounter a new situation or moral problem that they do not have the resources to address. When these kinds of doubt arise, a Christian responds faithfully by seeking clarity, new information, and answers to their questions. The process can be challenging, but it also can be life-giving. The presence of doubt can force believers to think more deeply about God, the world, their neighbors, and themselves.

They will have to make new decisions about their commitment to God and whether they will live in obedience to Christ. This process often results in a clarified set of convictions, renewed confidence in God, and a fresh commitment to a life of discipleship.

Second, God can use doubt to prepare Christians for future challenges. Many Christians grow up in the church and inherit their faith from their families. In such situations a life of faith seems natural, and intellectual and moral objections to Christianity may never be considered. This can result in faith that is more assumed than affirmed. Yet untested faith often collapses because the believer does not have the resources to respond when suffering or criticism comes. This is where a time of doubt can be helpful. God can use the experience of doubt to prepare Christians for difficult moments and give them the resources to respond. As Timothy Keller puts it, a "faith without doubts is like a human body without any antibodies in it."[8] Doubt produces strength for Christians precisely through the process of overcoming it. Facing doubt is difficult, and moving beyond it requires humility and courage in equal measure. The content of a Christian's faith becomes refined as old thought patterns are discarded and new ones formed. This process of purification enriches the Christian life by supplying the believer with new knowledge. It also can produce the sort of spiritual and emotional strength necessary to face difficult objections and overcome spiritual challenges. People who struggle through periods of doubt learn the valuable lessons that they will not always have all the answers and that they are not self-sufficient. They also learn that Christ walks alongside Christians in times of doubt and that Christ will be there at the end of the journey.

Third, God uses doubt to produce sympathy for others. The process of wrestling with doubt can be humiliating for a Christian. Many believers are taught that confidence and joy are the hallmarks of the Christian life. Their churches often are shaped by liturgies of praise that have little room for lament. As a result, Christians can feel out of place when doubt arises. Answers are no longer ready to hand, confidence is hard to come by, and joy has been replaced by confusion and anxiety. Questions and arguments against the faith that once seemed absurd now have new currency and relevance. This experience produces profound humility, but it also gives believers a new perspective on the people around them. They will have greater sympathy for those who simply cannot accept the claims of Christianity. Rather than flatly dismissing their objections to Christianity as absurd, the believer who had faced doubts will respect these arguments and the people making them. They also will show compassion for fellow believers who cannot muster the kind of confidence or joy considered by many to be normal. Christians who doubt not only will make room for these believers, but they also will seek to listen and learn from them. They will include their voices within their worship and see their contributions as vital to the church. God uses all of these things to foster charity within the Christian community. As the church expands its way of life to include those who do not fit the perceived template for a "good Christian," it also opens its mind to the insights of those outside the faith from which much might be learned.

HOW SHOULD THE CHURCH RESPOND TO DOUBTERS?

The Bible says directly: "Be merciful to those who doubt" (Jude 1:22). Showing mercy in this case means walking alongside someone with doubt as they work through their questions and problems. Christians sometimes pull away from doubters because the presence of doubt poses a challenge and brings discomfort. But a person dealing with doubt should never have to walk alone. Christians should seek out and embrace those who doubt with the goal not of fixing them but of loving and encouraging them.

When answers can be given to doubters' questions, Christians should seek to give them. They should work with and alongside those who doubt to address their concerns and point the way forward. Yet the proper response to a doubters' inquiries often is simply to listen to them. God is not challenged by the presence of doubt, and God does not need believers to rebuke doubters or immediately insist that they resolve their problems. Sometimes the best response to doubt is to hear what the person has to say, seek to understand their confusion, and then bear their burden alongside them (Gal 6:2). When pressed to give an answer to a difficult question, sometimes the proper response is to say, "I do not know." Above all, Christians can remain present in the lives of doubters. They can encourage the doubter to remain active in worship, remind them of the gospel, include them in the community, and serve them through concrete acts of love. In this way the church responds to doubters by directing them to Jesus Christ.

WHAT SHOULD I DO WHEN I DOUBT?

The first thing to do is recognize that doubt is a normal part of the Christian life. God is infinite, but humans are finite. A relationship with God will always stretch humans beyond their capacities, particularly when it comes to knowledge and understanding. Questions will arise that cannot be answered, and the resulting lack of clarity may produce doubt. Yet as Hebrews 11 shows, dealing with doubt is simply part of what it means to live a life of faith. When we read the stories of the figures mentioned in this passage, it becomes clear that all of them experienced times of uncertainty and doubt. When Noah built the ark, he did so to prepare for "events yet unseen" that did not seem probable (v. 7). Abraham left his home for a new land while "not knowing where he was going" (v. 8). Later, he faced the challenge of believing God's surprising promise that he would have many descendants "even though he was too old—and Sarah herself was barren" (v. 11). Moses risked Pharaoh's anger by leading the Israelites out of Egypt, and he did so even though he had not seen God directly and had doubts about his own abilities (v. 27). Without clear answers, these figures and many others felt like "strangers and foreigners on the earth" who were "seeking a homeland" they had yet to find (vv. 13-14). Many of them died without receiving everything God had promised them (vv. 13, 39).

The fact that the Bible presents these often-uncertain people as examples of faithfulness demonstrates that a life of faith can include periods of doubt. A helpful way to be reminded of this lesson is to read the Psalms. Many psalms offer exultant praise to God and express confidence in God's sovereign care and love. But many other psalms articulate feelings of confusion, loneliness, and betrayal: "O LORD, why do you cast me off? Why do you hide your face from me?" (Ps 88:14). Expressions of doubt like these have been used by God's people for centuries as part of their worship. They are expressions of faith in the midst of doubt, and they give Christians permission to offer similar expression to God. The Psalms serve as a training ground for Christians dealing with doubt. They teach believers to bring their uncertainties to God, with trust that doing so stands within God's will. God does not turn away from doubters but embraces them. He uses Scripture to provide doubters with language to help them bring their doubts to him.

For the Christian this looks like presenting doubts directly to Jesus, just as the father did in Mark 9. It is significant that after providing the list of the imperfect examples of faith, Hebrews concludes that believers should "run with perseverance" while always "looking to Jesus" (Heb 12:1-2). This is how Christians should respond to doubt: they should keep their eyes fixed on Jesus while trusting that Jesus will work alongside and within them to help them find confidence. Often, life with Christ in the midst of doubt looks like everyday discipleship. Dietrich Bonhoeffer argues that the first disciples of Jesus learned to follow Christ *before* they began to believe in him. "The road to faith passes through obedience to Christ's call," Bonhoeffer says. "Because we are justified by faith, faith and obedience have to be distinguished. But their division must never destroy their unity, which lies in the reality that faith exists only in obedience, is never without obedience. Faith is only faith in deeds of obedience."[9] A proper response to doubt is to live in obedience to Jesus. Sometimes a Christian's obedience *to* Christ will have to carry them along when they struggle to believe *in* Christ. Among many others things, a life of obedience includes activities of prayer, worship, service to one's neighbors, and love for one's enemies. These kinds of things can be done even in the midst of great doubt.

The first disciples serve as an example in this regard. Just before Christ gave them the Great Commission and sent them out to share the gospel to the world, Matthew notes that some of the disciples doubted Christ even as they worshiped him (Mt 28:17). The risen Jesus certainly knew about these disciples' doubt as they stood before him. But Christ did not pull back from them or ask them to figure everything out before they could begin to serve in his name. Their doubt did not disqualify them from their ministry. Instead, Christ looked directly at these doubters and then commissioned them. And as he did so, he made a promise that applies to every other doubter: "Remember, I am with you always, to the end of the age" (Mt 28:20).

Chapter Ten

Counseling

ELISHA EVELEIGH

LUCY IS A TEENAGE CLIENT I HAD A FEW YEARS AGO. By the time she arrived at my office, disheveled and droopy, she had experienced several episodes of depression that made it difficult for her to get out of bed all day. In addition to feeling suicidal at times, she also engaged in self-injury, had anxiety, and experienced panic attacks at school.

Many psychologists would not be surprised to hear that Lucy's mother also suffered from anxiety and depression, as well as her grandfather. Lucy's family regularly attended church, and she grew up going to Christian camps. Her parents were hesitant to seek psychological treatment for Lucy's symptoms but felt desperate to help their daughter. Initially, they took a valuable approach tried by many Christians and sought help from the church. They wondered if prayer, an improved spiritual life, and more faith might help Lucy feel better. She prayed, went to youth group when she could, read her Bible, and was aware of others praying for her.

Unfortunately, Lucy's symptoms continued to worsen, and she was hospitalized one night for feeling suicidal. Once she was stabilized, Lucy began weekly therapy sessions. In my office she described mounds of spiritual guilt about the fact that she continued to feel depressed. She wondered if God saw her, if he cared, if he was angry about something she did in the past.

Lucy told me how she went through life feeling numb and disinterested. She could not understand how her friends had the energy to care about school, sports, or relationships. She felt like a bad person at best, overlooked at worst, rejected by God. Mental health concerns like depression affect all of our relationships, including our view of God and the belief that he cares. Lucy needed a comprehensive approach to treatment. I believe the faith community plays an important role in the process of healing. I am also grateful for the development of effective, research-based mental health interventions. We implemented as many resources as needed to restore hope and normal functioning in Lucy's life. I still remember the day she walked into my office smiling and wearing a trendy teenage outfit. Her hair was curled, and she wanted to show me pictures of friends on her phone. She looked like a different person! For this and many other stories of God's transforming work, I am grateful. I wish that all such situations were resolved with such clarity and joy, but I know that's not always the case.

PRAYER, SCRIPTURE, AND COMMUNITY

Numerous aspects of faith can aid in coping with mental health concerns. Research on prayer, for instance, indicates a positive relationship between prayer and mental well-being. Additionally, faith communities offer important social connections that have been shown to benefit emotional well-being. Scripture explicitly supports the notion of seeking biblical truths and praying for God's intervention in times of distress. Indeed, Jesus invites all who are burdened and heavy laden to find rest in him (Mt 11:28). With the author of Lamentations, the Scriptures themselves provide comfort through meditation on God's promises or finding community in despair. Other sections of Scripture provide wisdom and useful direction for positive thinking. For instance, Philippians 4:8 urges us to think upon whatever is pure, lovely, admirable, or praiseworthy. Scripture is a rich source of comfort that many therapists use in their work. In the context of my work I have asked adolescents to meditate on Scriptures revealing God's love for them.

Although I believe God uses therapists in his healing work, there are numerous examples of Jesus providing spiritual, physical, and

emotional healing. I believe he can still do this today. My favorite biblical example of holistic renewal is the woman with the issue of blood
in Mark 5:25-34. Considering the cultural context of this story, the
woman must have lived a wretched life. She had been bleeding for
twelve years in a culture where she would have been considered ritually
unclean, as would anyone else who touched her. This would impede her
ability to take part in community life. The livelihood of women at that
time was significantly dependent on men, and being childless was a
source of shame. It is reasonable to assume, given her condition, this
woman may have lacked both a husband and children. Hence, she was
likely not wealthy, yet the Bible says she spent all she had, suffering a
great deal under the care of many doctors.

This was a woman full of shame, desperately seeking healing but
chained to suffering. I imagine that in a state of desperation she pushed
through the crowds, making people unclean left and right, convinced
that simply touching Jesus' clothes would heal her. It did. Jesus could
have just let the incident go and moved on. However, he desires healing
for the whole person. He demanded to know who touched him. Imagine
what it must have meant for a woman who spent twelve years as a suffering outcast to hear Jesus call her "daughter." He freed her from
shame and guilt, publicly commended her for her faith, and blessed her
to go in peace and be free from suffering. Through her faith in Jesus,
she was healed. The Lord continues to work spiritual, physical, and
emotional healing in our world and allows us to play a role through
prayer and faith.

Christian psychologists seek sources of strength in the life of a client,
and a prayerful community is certainly one of them. As a psychologist
I journey with a family, identifying and encouraging the skills they
need to function well. We also work together to set up natural sources
of support from family, friends, and faith communities. It is not my
intention to remain in the life of the family forever. In a way, the goal
of therapists is to put themselves out of business! I am grateful for the
time I spend with families but believe that God provides ongoing emotional support and healing from being richly connected with others.

Our individualist culture provides little help in this area. This is where the church community can play a significant role in caring for the souls of hurting individuals.

While the church provides critical support for individuals, pastors and other spiritual leaders have shared that they are sometimes over-whelmed by the mental health needs of their congregants. This may be an indication that the concerns are simply beyond their level of mental health training. In this case, it benefits both parties to refer individuals for more intensive mental health support. While most pastors are trained in counseling and the application of biblical truth to human flourishing, the Bible offers no simple cure for illnesses such as bipolar disorder. This may necessitate the addition of psychological treatment and medication to the community supports already in place. Doing so is not an issue of failed spirituality but of taking advantage of all the resources God provides to promote our well-being.

SIN, EVIL, AND EMOTIONAL SUFFERING

College students struggling with emotional pain have asked me whether personal sin or evil might be the cause of maladies like de-pression and anxiety. Sin and evil should be taken seriously when sitting with people in distress. This includes personal and systemic sin. Yet, given the proclivity of some in the church to blame people for emo-tional suffering, I seek to convey a thorough, balanced treatment of the topic. Throughout history people in various cultures have attributed mental health concerns to demon possession. This perspective goes in and out of vogue, following greater philosophical trends. Indeed, human history includes invasive techniques like trephination (making holes in the skull) to release evil spirits thought to be the source of mental illness. In Western societies evil continued as an explanation until the eighteenth century and pointed to witchcraft and demon-ology as the cause of mental illness. Unfortunately, these views fre-quently led to persecution and abuse for those with mental health concerns, as opposed to care and support.

Regarding the question of sin, it is necessary to consider both individual and systemic sources of sin. The latter includes things like racism and sexism. It is understandable that a student might wonder about the impact of sin on mental health functioning. Even in Scripture, we see the disciples asking Jesus whether a man's blindness was due to his own sin or that of his parents (Jn 9:1-2). It seems that many Christians are willing to accept the fact that diabetes or cancer may not be tied to personal sin but have doubts when it comes to mental health.

When students ask about the link between personal sin and mental health, I tell them that if they are involved in a spree of bank robberies, then legitimate anxiety symptoms may result from concerns about getting caught. Fear and anxiety might be a natural consequence of bank robbing behaviors. Another example is when a person involved in an inappropriate sexual relationship may begin to feel shame and develop depressive symptoms. I mention these scenarios to demonstrate that it is possible to engage in behaviors that lead to or exacerbate mental health concerns. However, to make the broad statement that all mental health concerns are the result of personal sin is too simplistic and even offensive to those who suffer but are no more sinful than the average person.

Numerous factors besides personal sin correlate with increased risk for mental health problems. According to the National Alliance on Mental Illness, 18.5 percent of adults in the United States experience mental illness in a given year. Given that all of us sin, it is clear that complex issues are at play in the development of mental health concerns. For instance, medical issues like hypothyroidism, Parkinson's disease, or neurotransmitter performance are correlated with mental health concerns. For example, the level of hormones produced by the thyroid gland can be a factor in depression. In this case, treating the thyroid might be more effective for relieving depressive symptoms than using psychotherapy to directly address the depression.

Factors such as family dynamics, societal problems, loneliness, and some cultural values (e.g., materialism) play a clear role in human well-being. Christians considering the link between sin and mental

illness would benefit from studying the impact of systemic or institutional sin on negative emotional experiences. Racism, for example,
goes beyond individual negative beliefs, attitudes, and behaviors
against minorities by involving larger institutions and cultural norms
that result in negative outcomes. Research suggests, for instance,
that perceived racism is associated with symptoms of depression,
anxiety, deceased well-being, lower self-worth, and more physical
health concerns.[1] Another factor impacting mental health is childhood
problems like parental divorce, unsupportive parents, or abuse. Such
experiences can disrupt the attachment bond between the child and
parents resulting in relational and emotional challenges throughout
the life span.

Churches are frequently on the front lines of mental health care and
should make efforts to destigmatize mental health concerns, providing guilt-free space for contemplating suffering, spiritual doubt,
and despair. Vulnerability requires the development of a trustworthy
community where mental health concerns are not silenced or overlooked. It is reductionistic to say that mental health problems result
from personal sin and that simple individual repentance of wrong-
doing will always heal us from all emotional and relational concerns
without the need for further work. It is also reductionistic to believe
that all emotional and relational concerns are simply physiological or
psychological and can be cured without addressing individual and systemic grievances. Such views can be a hindrance to healing and growth.
I believe that a whole-person approach is best. We must pray for empathy and spiritual insight when we seek to encourage our fellow
Christians in spiritual growth without loading on counterproductive
spiritual guilt.

SEEKING A COUNSELOR

When my previous roommate's aunt found out she was living with a
psychology professor (me), she became worried that the faith of my
roommate, Emma, would be corrupted. Emma explained that I was a
Christian and gave her aunt a rundown of all my faith-related

activities—an attempt to prove that my association with the field of psychology had not somehow contaminated my faith. Still, Emma's aunt was suspicious. Skepticism remains among some Christians as to whether psychology is a valid, helpful means to address the mental health of believers. How could a field that is historically pessimistic toward religion, one whose theories are sometimes in contrast with Christian perspectives be useful for easing emotional pain?

A 2013 poll by Lifeway Research found that one-third of Americans and half of evangelicals, fundamentalists, and born-again Christians believe that serious mental illness can be cured by prayer and Bible study alone. Christians who argue against the use of psychology are frequently responding to the underlying assumptions of various movements or theories in the field. For instance, behaviorism overlooks the mind and spirit, atomizes humans, and assumes a deterministic perspective of human functioning. A Humanistic approach could be critiqued for assuming that we are the sole masters of our destiny, rejecting other sources of authority.

Asking whether we can turn to psychology for answers is steeped in the bigger question about epistemology (the study of knowledge). We must ask whether the empirical practices of social science research are a valid means to discover useful information about human functioning and growth. My confidence is based on the intent of Christian researchers in the field of psychology to discover or observe what God already knows about factors influencing human functioning.

As a Christian I trust that the world created by God is observable and knowable. God has equipped human beings to take up scientific research in order to gain knowledge and understanding of the natural world, including the psychological complexity of human beings. This is why we can explore the world and every science with confidence, knowing that the truths we discover point back to the same God who created all that we have. No corner of God's world is off-limits to our study.

Psychology is a social science, and our research involves empirical practices. Through this research we understand that restoration of life with each other and with God is an essential feature of the ongoing renewal of our lives (2 Cor 5:18). The Bible calls this "reconciliation," and it is not only a work accomplished by God's grace found in Jesus Christ, but it is a work that continues in our hearts through the activity of the Holy Spirit.

I am astounded that God chose to use humans like you and me in his work of healing bodies, souls, emotions, and relationships. Does God participate in the restoration of our broken lives? Yes. But God also uses the gifts and training of professionals to participate with him in healing. In the field of psychology, much of this training is based on theory and empirical evidence that we integrate with our Christian view of persons to care for those that God brings into our offices. What a blessing to be in community, used by God to help one another.

Therefore, let me be bold and perfectly clear: if you (or anyone you know) is suffering from depression, anxiety, or any other illness that is robbing you of the life you've always wanted, or if you (or a friend) are experiencing suicidal thoughts, yes indeed, pray and seek spiritual support. But do not be reluctant to seek professional help. Many people seek medical attention for physical illnesses such as broken bones or diabetes even though they believe in the healing power of God. If you're thinking or your emotions are causing suffering that you cannot explain, seek help as well. Seeking help is not a sign of weakness or a lack of faith—it is a sign of maturity and courage.

INTEGRATING PSYCHOLOGY AND FAITH

There is a lively debate among Christian counselors seeking good techniques for addressing mental health concerns. Whereas a pastoral counselor will help people based on scriptural insights alone, a professional therapist asks whether we can know anything from the field of psychology that aids us in helping people. Christian psychologists use the term *integration* to describe the careful application of psychology within the framework of the doctrines many Christians subscribe to. Those who support integrative work agree that there is no one approach to the practice of psychology as a believer. They also agree that the term *integration* is imperfect, given that there is no need to integrate the knowledge researchers discover about humans (created by God) with a godly perspective. Nevertheless—given the historical debate and ongoing questions from both sides regarding whether the two are compatible, the term remains.

Many fine pieces have been written on how Christian psychologists might faithfully use theoretical approaches from the field of psychology. This requires a thorough appraisal of the approach to identify areas of overlap and disagreement. In their book *Modern Psychotherapies*, Stan Jones and Rich Butman provide the following model for assessing the underpinning of theoretical approaches:

- Attend to the *philosophical assumptions* of each approach to counseling. This includes ideas about human character and agency. What is the perspective on personhood, truth, realty, purpose, and so on? Are the consequences of the fall and the reality of evil taken seriously?

- Examine the *model of personality* upon which the approach is built. How are human motivations understood? What are the explicit or implicit core human characteristics?

- Consider the *model of abnormality* or how the problem came to be. Is the approach compatible with the Christian faith? This includes concepts like human accountability and whether there is a balance between personal causation of distress (resulting from our own sins) and systemic causation of distress (living in a fallen world). Are Christian virtues viewed as abnormal?

- The *model of health* is also important—what does it look like to be emotionally whole and healthy?

- What is the *model of psychotherapy* or *methods of change* and growth? Do the methods provide resources for healing that are consistent with biblical truth and wisdom? Are agape love and compassion employed while acknowledging contextual factors?

- Does the approach have *demonstrated effectiveness* to promote good stewardship of resources and time?[2]

I use a similar model developed along with my colleague Terri Watson when teaching psychological theories to undergraduate students. We highlight the importance of *applied* integration to address individual and systemic problems. We also hope that integration fosters enthusiasm for compassionate justice resulting in *advocacy* for the underserved and marginalized. In my own practice of integration, I often feel like the psychological theory is a piece of tracing paper that I lay over my Christian view of humans. I can always see my foundational values showing through the paper, influencing how I apply the approach.

SECULAR COUNSELORS

All licensed secular counselors are trained in professional therapeutic techniques and therefore offer growth and healing in clients. They are aware of the ways that the brain, social factors, and personal circumstances influence human functioning, and they have experience implementing effective interventions. And as a part of their training they learn to respect the worldview and spiritual commitments of their clients. A good secular counselor should not dismantle your faith.

But Christian counselors also provide effective therapy for individuals with differing belief systems. Of course, the Christian therapist's worldview stays the same, just as the perspectives of a secular therapist remain intact when working with Christian clients. Christian views such as God's design for our life and Jesus' command to love our neighbors allow believing therapists to view clients with an immense amount of value irrespective of individual circumstances, life preferences, or religious affiliation. In one instance I was treating a teenage girl, whose family practiced Hinduism, for a problem called school refusal. This means that she was afraid to attend school and even struggled to think about her school. Hinduism is a religion with deep cultural roots and practices, and I respected the family, their culture, and their beliefs. During our first session, I asked the family to complete an intake form that included a place to indicate whether they would like faith explicitly integrated into their treatment. They said no. I was happy to proceed with a behavioral intervention that included systematic desensitization. Little by little the client was exposed to the school setting. First by having the name of the school on a white board in my office, then by imagining sitting in class. Later, she drove by the school, then pulled in the parking lot, and left. Meanwhile, she worked on her many depressive symptoms. I am grateful to report that research-based therapy techniques had great results for this client. Her depressive symptoms improved, and she returned to school full-time. She also felt inspired by the field of psychology and became an advocate for mental health awareness among adolescents in the area, speaking at local schools and leading a group.

A secular therapist in this situation would have likely seen similar results. However, depending on the reasons for counseling, it is important to determine what value there may be in working with a therapist who shares similar beliefs. Secular counselors lack the benefit of having thought through the integration of Christian faith and psychology. There are many fine training programs that explicitly teach this integration. In my own training I found myself filtering the theories and approaches through my Christian worldview. I thought about whether the ideas seemed to be in line with Scripture and a Christian view of persons. I am grateful for the body of integration literature that facilitated this task (see writings by Mark McMinn, Stan Jones, and Mark Yarhouse, for example).[3]

The field of psychology is dominated by secular therapists. Yet secular therapy lacks an understanding of Christian hope.[4] This hope can be a major factor in resilience and is predicated on our standing before and relationship with a loving God. This is one of many examples of how believers may benefit from working with a therapist who shares a similar understanding of the gospel.

MEDICATION AND FAITH

Psychologists who work in counseling and psychiatrists, who are medical doctors, both consider the interaction of complex factors to determine whether medication might be warranted. In some cases medication is precisely what is needed because the problem is primarily biological. These professionals analyze the nature of the problem, its origins, the person's genetics, and brain-based influences that may affect emotional issues. Problems such as marital trouble, unhelpful thinking patterns, or destructive coping mechanisms may not require medical intervention. However, physiological dysfunction could play a role in each of these situations. During an initial intake interview, psychologists ask about the family's history of mental illness, family dynamics, and coping strategies. This gives us insight into the extent to which genetics may be contributing to the presenting problems versus modeling of poor coping mechanisms. For instance, an individual who has a family member with depression is five times more likely to develop the disorder. Additionally, a child who witnesses his father's fear of elevators can learn that elevators are unsafe and develop a similar fear. It is challenging to fully understand what environmental or biological factors might be involved.

Opponents of medical treatment for emotional pain remind us that suffering can lead to the development of positive character traits such as perseverance and compassion. Indeed, life's trails can strengthen faith and hope. Wisdom is required to discern when suffering might result in growth and when it is appropriate to take advantage of the resources to alleviate suffering. But we have to be careful here so that we do not endorse or sustain suffering because we think we are promoting spiritual benefits.

Mental illness is a complex medical issue that can result from various interrelated influences. Often in addressing mental health issues people ask the basic question of nature or nurture. The quick answer is both. Research has demonstrated that nature and nurture reciprocally influence one another. A popular model for understanding the onset of mental health concerns is the *diathesis-stress model*. This is the idea that a person may have a biological predisposition to a mental or physical health disorder and social factors can increase the likelihood of symptoms developing. For instance, if two people are predisposed to have an anxiety disorder and only one of them is exposed to a traumatic event, that person may be more likely to develop symptoms than the person living in stable conditions.

It is widely known that disorders like schizophrenia and bipolar disorder have a strong tie to neurotransmitter functioning. Simply put, things are not working right in the brain. Individuals with schizophrenia, for example, have excessive levels of dopamine or oversensitive dopamine receptors. Brain differences, such as enlarged ventricles (cavities filled with cerebrospinal fluid) and hypofrontality (decreased activity in the frontal lobe of the brain) are also implicated when an individual has schizophrenia. In addition to changes in brain function and structure, research involving twins and siblings reveals interesting results regarding the genetic links of the disorder. In identical twins, if one twin has schizophrenia, the other twin is forty-eight times more likely than the general population to develop the disorder. In fraternal twins the number is seventeen times. If a person's nontwin sibling has schizophrenia, that person is ten times more likely than the general population to have the disorder. Understanding biological factors informs how medication may be a helpful tool in addressing mental health symptoms. For disorders like schizophrenia, a comprehensive treatment approach that includes medication to regulate brain functioning is often necessary to diminish symptoms and enable the client to participate in counseling. Knowing the genetic influence on the development of mental health conditions deters me from assuming that mental health conditions can simply be attributed to an individual's failed spirituality.

Overall, counseling has been shown to have positive benefits. Students frequently ask whether everyone would benefit from going to counseling. Given the advent of positive psychology, which seeks to build on strengths and cultivate virtue, there is something to be gained for anyone seeking to grow. Indeed, many Christian psychologists advocate for a perspective of therapy as caring for the soul as opposed to offering a cure, per se. For believers, counseling can be a helpful addition to the support provided by friends, family, and the church. The wisdom of our counselors and the sound training of our doctors can help us take back lives that seem to be slipping out of control. When we take advantage of these resources, hope can return. And with hope we can begin to gain a sense of purposefulness and happiness that we have not felt for years.

Chapter Eleven

Religious Pluralism

DAVID B. CAPES

FOR THE LAST FIFTEEN YEARS I have found myself in one of the most unexpected places I could imagine. I have been a cohost on a radio show that airs on one of the largest secular networks in the United States. It is called "A Show of Faith," and for about two hours I sit with two friends—a Roman Catholic priest and a Jewish rabbi—talking about life and religion. Imagine. An evangelical, a priest, and a rabbi all at the same microphone.

The mission of the show is to discuss events in the news from the standpoints of our faiths. A secondary mission is to demonstrate that people can be friends across faiths. In a time of widespread social polarization, as we have today, we think there is good value there. Over the years we have had Muslims, Jews, Hindus, Buddhists, various Christians, agnostics, Baha'is and others as guests. At that time I have learned a great deal. More importantly, I consider my cohosts, Father Mario Arroyo, a Cuban-born Catholic priest, and Rabbi Stuart Federow, leader of a conservative Jewish congregation south of Houston, to be dear friends.

APATHY AND OUTRAGE

Why do people respond to religious beliefs with either apathy or outrage, and why can't we just have a friendly dialogue about what we believe?

These days it seems people respond to authentic expressions of faith with either apathy ("Whatever") or outrage ("How dare you?"). The latter, of course, is not really a question; it is an accusation. Both responses may be the result of what has become the dominant "religion" in America, especially among millennials; scholars call it *moralistic therapeutic deism*. Any student of religion these days recognizes this is not an American perspective; it is a Western perspective. Two sociologists of religion, Christian Smith and Melinda Lundquist Denton, coined the phrase after spending a few years interviewing thousands of teenagers.[1] They came up with five beliefs that appear to describe a popular new "religion" emerging in America:

- There is a god who created and ordered the world; this god watches over humanity from a distance.
- This god wants us to be nice, good, and fair to one another just like most religions teach.
- The goal of life is to be happy and feel good about ourselves.
- This god gets involved only when we need god to solve a problem.
- Good people go to heaven when they die.

Now if these beliefs actually describe what a majority of young people think today, then it makes sense why they respond to other truth claims with apathy or outrage. Apathy arises when a person hears someone making a truth claim and then dismisses it as irrelevant to them for a variety of reasons. After all, there are so many religions. How are we going to distinguish between them? If we can't, then there is no reason to try. And why would we? We want to live in a tolerant world, don't we?

But tolerance is not the same thing as apathy. I'm not apathetic when the temperatures fall in Chicago to 25 degrees below zero, but I do tolerate them. You can't tolerate something you find pleasant or agreeable, or something you don't have any opinion about. You can only be tolerant of something that makes you deeply uncomfortable. Apathy means I don't care one way or another. Tolerance means I am willing to live with and work through the discomfort. I don't know about you, but I don't want to live in an apathetic age.

Outrage arises when people hear someone making a truth claim and it offends them deeply. They don't share that belief and find it contemptable that anyone would believe it, in the first place, and then anyone would be willing to tell others. They feel they should live in a space where only their ideas and thoughts are agreed to and affirmed. To be fair, we live in an age of outrage because there is a lot that should make us angry: terrorism, sex trafficking, the human and financial cost of wars and civil unrest around the world, injustice, and racism. But when we stand ready to be offended by anything, the chances are good we will find it.

Rather than apathy and outrage, the better posture toward different religions and beliefs should be one of respectful dialogue. It is respectful because every human being we encounter is made in the image and likeness of God. That alone is enough to say, "I respect you" and "I will treat you with respect." It is dialogue because it involves two people (at least) speaking and listening. I don't mean pretending to listen; I mean actually listening. We often want to speak and make our points. We ought to be able to speak, but often that right first has to be earned by developing a listening heart. Respectful dialogue does not say, "It's so quaint that you think that" or "I am deeply offended that you hold that." At the same time, respectful dialogue does not mean agreement. You may disagree deeply with what someone has said, and yet when both parties walk away they will sense they have been heard and respected. When we reach that point, there is a good chance we will be welcomed to share what we believe.

This reminds me of the second part of the peace prayer associated with Francis of Assisi (c. AD 1181–1226). Here we have a model of the sort of temperament that makes for respectful dialogue:

> O Master, let me not seek as much
> to be consoled as to console,
> to be understood as to understand,
> to be loved as to love,
> for it is in giving that one receives,

it is in self-forgetting that one finds,

it is in pardoning that one is pardoned,

it is in dying that one is raised to eternal life.[2]

St. Francis is setting before us a very high goal. Imagine if as citizens of our nation or as members of our churches we decided that it was more important to understand others than to demand that they understand us. It is hard to be outraged when someone insists on truly listening to us. It is also difficult to be apathetic when people are listening to us carefully with deep respect.

ARE ALL RELIGIONS THE SAME?

I often get asked, "Aren't all religions basically the same?" It is a good question, an important question, one that we need to consider. People often describe our search for God (or everlasting life) like a mountain. There are many ways up that mountain, and yet not all ways are the same. You can approach the mountain from the east or west, north or south. You can take the steep or more gradual incline. In the end, according to this way of thinking, all paths arrive at the summit with God.

I like this analogy for several reasons. First, it recognizes that there is something in all humans that points us to God. St. Augustine, addressing God says, "You have made us for yourself, and our heart is restless until it rests in you."[3] Peter Kreeft calls this one of the greatest sentences ever written.[4] We are all wired the same way, to think about God, to seek purpose and meaning in life, and eventually to find our way to God. This is true of all people of all time, as various disciplines like archaeology, anthropology, sociology, and religious studies demonstrate. Second, it recognizes that there are important common features of nearly all religions. As you get to know "true believers" of other religions, we discover aspects that are similar. That doesn't erase the differences, but it at least helps us situate the other person and their faith. Third, it describes the ascent to God as a "way." I like that image because the earliest followers of Christ also referred to their lives as following "the Way" long before anyone called them "Christians"

(Acts 9:2; 19:23; 22:4). The reason they did so probably had to do with specific teachings of John the Baptizer and Jesus. Fourth, there is something about a mountain that casts our gaze to the heavens. Whether we are at its base or its peak, we experience a sense of awe and transcendence. These are universal experiences. It is the reason why people built temples on high places.

Eventually of course all analogies break down, including this one. Any significant mountain cannot be climbed in fourteen different ways. I know several people who decided they would climb Mt. Kilimanjaro, the highest mountain in Africa. They didn't stand at its base and say to each other, "You take the north face. I'll take the west, and we will see you at the top." Mountains must be approached with caution, training, the right equipment, a good guide, and by a designated, studied path. Not all ways will lead to the summit. Some will end in disaster or frustration. In fact, in many cases, there is only one way to the top.

The question of whether all religions are the same is more complicated than it seems. You can't simply answer yes or no. Perhaps it might be better to break it down into several subquestions to clarify what is meant by the same. Do all religions refer to the same supernatural being, higher power, or God? Do all religions lead to the same afterlife? Do all religions encourage the same ethical life? Each of these questions would take an entire essay to sort out. My point here is to say that what seem to be simple questions are not simple at all: often they have complex answers that are worth considering.

Let's consider the first question: Do all religions refer to the same supernatural being, higher power, or God? A part of the problem is the word *God* (in English). Every religion I am aware of uses the word *God* but means something different by it. My Catholic friend Father Mario Arroyo is fond of saying the word *God* is like an empty box; we have to put something in it to know what we've got. If we begin looking closely, every religion that uses *God* to speak of the supreme power puts something different in the box. Christians, for example, cannot think of God apart from Jesus, the Son of God, and the Holy Spirit, the second and third Persons of the Trinity. Yet Judaism and Islam disagree. According to their views, there is no Trinity, and as Muslim and Jewish friends tell me, "Jews and Muslims have more in common than with Christians because at least we are monotheists. Christians are polytheists." Now, I would disagree with that characterization; I say we too are monotheists. The point is that Jews, Christians, Muslims, Buddhists, Hindus, Daoists (the list goes on) all put something different in the box when it comes to *God*. Even within a religion, there are disagreements. I've had Hindu friends tell me that there are thousands of gods in Hinduism, and others tell me there is one God with many manifestations. I know Buddhists who believe in God and yet others are agnostic to the question; for them religion is about something else altogether. So if someone comes to us and asks, "Do all religions believe in the same God"? we have to ask the question, "What do you mean by *God*? What does your God box have in it?" It's never good to answer a complicated question yes or no. It is far better to stand back and ask clarifying questions if we really want to understand.

Now we could do the same thing with the other two questions: Do all religions lead to the same afterlife? Do all religions encourage the same ethical life? Again, answer a question with a question: What do you mean by *afterlife*? or What goes under the category of an *ethical life*? When we dig down into each question, we realize it is more complicated than it seems. Even Christians have different views of the afterlife. Some believe that the fate of the wicked is eternal suffering in hell; others think their fate is annihilation. Some Christians think that at death a person sleeps (in Jesus) until the second coming of the Lord, yet others hold that the believer who dies is immediately present with Christ. Some Jews will say they do not believe in an afterlife at all. When a person is dead, they are dead. Full stop! Other Jews say yes we do have a view of the afterlife, but it is distinct from what Christians believe. My rabbi friend says he believes in hell but does not believe anyone is actually there. The goal of Buddhism is not to "die and go to heaven," as Christians often say, but to reach nirvana, a state of being that is beyond striving, desiring, and suffering, released from the cycle of birth, death, and rebirth.

Consider just one aspect of the ethical life, that is, our diets. Jews and Muslims are scrupulous about their diets, not eating pork and insisting that their food be kosher or halal. Kosher and halal have to do with how the animals in our food are killed. They must be killed in the most merciful way possible, and they must be healthy at the time of death. Many Christians say a blessing before a meal, but never give a thought to how the pig was slaughtered. *Ahimsa* is an important feature of Jainism, an ancient religion of India; for Jains, all living things are sacred and must be treated with respect. Therefore, they do no harm to animals or insects. So, as you might guess, they do not eat meat. In fact, a Zoroastrian friend once told me, "When you eat meat, your stomach is the graveyard of animals." That's a rather disturbing image. Now to be fair, there are Christians who are vegetarians or vegans because of their Christian convictions. When it comes to refusing to drink alcohol, perhaps the best known are Mormons and Muslims. According to both faiths, a true believer must abstain from alcohol on moral grounds. Some Christians hold to that standard; others do not. I hope I've given you enough here to think that not all religions think of the good life or the ethical life the same way. There are important distinctions.

In the end, the answer to whether all religions are the same has to be answered with a nuanced no. There are important similarities between many faiths that we can seek to understand when we decide to love our neighbor who practices a different faith. But we need to grapple too with the stark differences between our faiths.

AM I MISSING SOMETHING BY NOT HAVING FRIENDS OF OTHER FAITHS?

If you live in some rural areas of the United States, the chances are good that you will not find many people of other faiths. There are exceptions, of course. But if you live in some of the cities, opportunities abound to meet, work with, and get to know people of other faiths. Just one example: Chicago is the kind of city in which over two hundred languages are spoken every day before breakfast. We might go to work and speak English or Spanish, but the languages of our homes and dreams are in the hundreds. With language goes culture. At the heart of culture is religion. Language, culture, and religion are deeply intertwined. In rural places, houses of worship may be limited to churches of various denominations. But in and around America's largest cities there are churches, synagogues, temples, and mosques where the coreligionists gather regularly to worship, study, and form communities.

It is possible, however, to live in a large city but have limited contact with people of other faiths. We might go to a private Christian school and be surrounded most of the time by people like us. We can live in cultural isolation despite our cosmopolitan surroundings. But we can choose to engage our context and richly benefit from friendships with people from other faiths. These encounters do not simply happen; they need to be actively pursued.

There are wonderful benefits here. When we get to know a person who practices another faith, it brings our own faith into focus. Over time, our knowledge of our own faith begins to grow. As my rabbi friend is fond of saying, "He who knows only one faith knows none." The Christians I know who have the best handle on who they are and what they believe have at some point juxtaposed their own faiths over against another (or others). It is in that compare-and-contrast mode that clear lines come into focus.

The same dynamic is at play in other areas of knowledge. For nearly twenty-five years I have taught undergraduate and graduate students New Testament Greek. After studying Greek with me for a year or more, most people will say, "I have learned more about English and how my language works in your Greek class than I ever learned in high school." Other Greek teachers have told me their students say the same thing. When we study a second language, know its forms, and how it works, then it puts our own language into sharper focus. If all we do is to study English, the chances are good we'll never understand fully how it works. The same is true in other areas of life. If all we know is our own faith, and we never put it side by side with another, it could well be that our own spiritual growth could be stunted. There are personal benefits to having friends of other faiths.

But there is a second reason that goes back to the scriptural command "Love your neighbor as yourself" (Lev 19.18; Mt 22.37-40). How can we love our Muslim, Jewish, and other neighbors if we do not know who they are or what they hold dear? I'm afraid much of what we know about other religions comes from cable news, sketchy websites, and people with an agenda. In other words, what we know is often not true. By having friends of other faiths, we can get to know the truth of who they are and what they believe. But relationships like these do not come easily or mature quickly. It takes time.

David Kinnaman and Gabe Lyon discuss in their book *unChristian* how Christians often are quick to judge others.[5] These followers of Jesus believe (wrongly) that they know the "other" and have all the answers. It's a disposition deeply ingrained in us and hard to root out. But if we are going to truly love our neighbors and be able to bear witness faithfully to God and the gospel, we have to know them on their own terms, not someone else's. We don't love everyone in general without loving someone in particular. That particularity is messy. So Kinnaman and Lyon offer some good counsel on how to develop relationships of respect between Christians and non-Christians. I summarize them here:

1. Listen more, talk less. You may learn something important.

2. Don't label people or try to fit them into neat, little boxes.

3. Don't pretend to have all the answers. Be willing to say, "I don't know."

4. Put yourself in the other's place.

5. Be authentic. Recognize when you are trying to push your own agenda.

6. Be a true friend with no other motives. Don't make people your "project."[6]

This is good counsel if we hope to establish meaningful relationships with people of other faiths. But there is one more benefit. You may find yourself truly enjoying their company. They are interesting and fascinating people. Some of my lifelong friends have been friends of other faiths.

WILL I COMPROMISE MY FAITH IF I STUDY OTHER RELIGIONS?

I have met people and heard stories of those who studied other religions and gave up on the faith. But I don't know whether one was the cause of the other. People, for reasons other than studying world religions, walk away from their faith. So yes, it can happen, but it is not inevitable. I have met a lot of people who have had the opposite experience; as I suggested earlier, when we study other religions our own faith is enriched and comes into focus.

When I think of someone who studied religions and myths of the ancient world and stayed a vibrant Christian, I think first of C. S. Lewis. In fact, it is safe to say that studying the myths and religions of the past helped him return to the faith of his youth.[7] In *Mere Christianity* Lewis writes:

> If you are a Christian you do not have to believe that all the other religions are simply wrong all through. If you are an atheist you do have to believe that the main point in all religions of the whole world is simply one huge mistake. If you are a Christian, you are free to think that all those religions, even the queerest ones, contain at least some hint of the truth. When as an atheist I had to try and persuade myself that most of the human race have always been wrong about the question that mattered to them the most; when I became a Christian I was able to take a more liberal [generous] view.[8]

Lewis found a bit of truth in all religions, even the odd ones, apparently. But we can't know that truth if we have already prejudged that all religions are wrong, top to bottom. According to Lewis, before we study them we should not prejudge them; and as we study them, it's best not to judge them either. Rather, look for the light they contain. As I have written elsewhere: "Since God is light and in Him there is no darkness, any light visible in other religions—no matter how faint or flickering—must be attributed to Him."[9]

In his famous essay "Myth Became Fact," Lewis remarks that we ought not to be surprised to find parallels and typologies of Christ in other religions.[10] It would be odd if we did not because all people of all ages yearn for transcendence, beauty, purpose, and truth. Lewis's lifelong interest lay in the dying-rising gods of some of the world's most ancient religions. To be clear, Lewis asserted that the full flowering of faith is found only in Jesus Christ—his incarnation, life, death, and resurrection—the "true myth," yet we see hints of that fullness and desires for it in the literature the ancients have left behind. Those texts underwrite all the world religions. As Lewis expert Michael Ward writes, "Paganism contained a good deal of meaning that was realized, consummated and perfected in Christ."[11] So Lewis stands as a great example of someone who worked closely with other myths, stories, and religions of the world and came away with a sharper focus on truth. I don't think anyone could ever criticize Lewis for having watered down the faith.

My advice would be to study these other religions and continually ask these questions: What does this teaching or practice say about who we are as human beings and our deepest desires? What image of God emerges from this faith? How does this religion envision all that appears to be wrong in the world? What sort of future and life does this religion project? These are fundamental questions of theology and philosophy. Every religion deals with them differently. By studying these questions we can wrestle with them and be prepared to return to our own Christian faith afresh with a new set of eyes and questions. When we do, we will find an opportunity for growth and understanding.

HOW DO WE SHARE OUR FAITH IN A PLURALISTIC CULTURE/WORLD?

One of the most significant questions we ask is: How are Christians supposed to share their faith in a pluralistic world? It is a hard question to answer given the realities we face today.

A part of the problem is our starting point. In thinking about sharing our faith, most people's first thoughts run to *talking*: What do I say? How do I say it? When? Well, what if that is the wrong starting point? What if the right starting point is not about talking but about *listening* and *observing*? Until we truly listen to others and what they have to say, until we take notice of their ways and God's ways in the world, I'm not sure we will know what to say and how to say it.

I take as my model here the apostle Paul and how he dealt with the people of Athens (Acts 17:16-34). Athens was a religiously complex city and deemed as one of the most sophisticated cities of its day. The city was filled with temples; many gods were worshiped in shrines and honoring these gods was a normal gesture of daily life. This was commonplace throughout the Roman Empire, and we might imagine using the modern term *religious pluralism* to describe these Roman cities.

The Athenians were curious people; they loved philosophy and religious debate. Paul was there long enough and developed enough of a reputation among the inquisitive leaders that one day they invited him to speak at the Areopagus, a platform where the curious gathered for speeches, discussions, and, on occasion, debates.

Part of Paul's missionary strategy was to develop common ground with his audiences. In the synagogues that meant quoting from the law and the prophets and showing how Jesus fulfilled the unresolved hopes and promises of the Hebrew Scriptures. In Greco-Roman contexts like Athens that meant closely observing the literature and religious actions of the people. In Acts 17:22-28 we probably do not have an exact transcript of the speech that day, but we have a good summary from Luke of what Paul said. The apostle began by observing the strong and diverse religious ethos of the city. He commended them over and over for being a "religious" people. He talked about how he had walked their streets, considering their statues and reading their inscriptions. On one of his walks he found a shrine dedicated to an unknown God. For Paul, that was the perfect way to introduce the Creator God and Jesus to them.

Rather than judging the Athenians and criticizing them for being completely wrong about gods and religions, Paul sought common ground. He spent time with them, watched them, observed them, appreciated them, and ultimately commended them for what he found. But Paul went a step further. He began quoting lines from their own poets. He had taken time to listen and memorize key lines from some of their poets and prophets.

How many of us have spent the time to read, study, and in some cases memorize lines from the Qur'an, Bhagavad Gita, or the writings of Confucius, the sacred writings of those around us? To do so shows respect for them and will in most cases earn us a right to speak. Paul quoted Epimenides, a sixth-century BC Greek poet: "In him we live and move and have our being" (Acts 17:28). For Epimenides the god he referred to was Zeus, but Paul turned it around and made it a reference to the one, true God of creation. Then the apostle quoted a line from Aratus, a Greek poet of the third century BC: "We are his offspring" (v. 28). Again, Aratus likely had Zeus in mind when he penned those words, but Paul redirected it to refer to God the Father. The apostle to the Gentiles is respectfully suggesting that the god they called "unknown" and Zeus—as well as other gods for that matter—is known to us finally and definitively as God, the Father of the Lord Jesus Christ—the God who created all things and who raises the dead.

Now if we read on, we realize that Paul's witness in Athens was not completely successful. Ultimately, he did speak up, share the gospel, and make claims that were rejected by most of his audience. A few became believers, but others mocked his claim that Jesus had been raised from the dead (vv. 32-34). This part of the message was a serious impediment to Gentile conversions. Even as Paul sought common ground with the Athenians, he did not shy away from affirming the extraordinary truth of the resurrection. He trusted in the inherent power of the gospel. Elsewhere Paul insists that his calling is not to develop missionary strategies that rely on his ability to persuade. He understands his calling to "proclaim the gospel, and not with eloquent wisdom, so that the cross of Christ might not be emptied of its power" (1 Cor 1:17 NRSV). Paul trusted in the power of the cross and resurrection. I learned a long time ago that I cannot predict or control how people respond to my witness to Christ. I learned that my basic task is simply to share Christ with others in the power of the Holy Spirit.

Finally, let me add another thought. If we want to be effective in sharing the gospel in a religiously pluralistic world, it is not enough for us to speak about Christ. We must be conformed to Christ and not to the ways of this world (Rom 12:1-2). We must become like Jesus. And we cannot do that alone. We do that only in community. As Michael Gorman says, we must become the gospel.[12] God's mission must become our mission and purpose. When we do more than just believe the good news, we allow it to take shape in us; this is ultimately how we participate in the life and mission of God.

CONCLUSION

The future of our world will be increasingly pluralistic. Political, cultural, and religious boundaries are becoming increasingly permeable as our lives become more global and as the internet introduces us to people and ideas that were unknowable just seventy-five years ago. Standing in the center of this pluralism with a dynamic and resilient Christian faith will be no easy task. It will require that we become sympathetic listeners to others and ready to make new friends. We will discover much that we have in common but also that we have much that sets our faith apart. But ultimately we will need to know our Christian faith well and remember that it is Jesus Christ—the unique revelation of the one true God—who is essential for understanding God, our world, and ourselves rightly.

Chapter Twelve

Activism

MATT VEGA

ALMOST EVERY WEEK MY INBOX IS FILLED with requests for coffee. Pastors, college students, professors, and parents all want to know what the life of an activist is like and how one should think about it from a Christian perspective. It's hard to approach the topic because I'm never sure where to begin. People are all over the place in their spiritual journeys. I have two types of friends: some who can't talk about activism enough, and others who have an allergy to the slightest whiff of "social justice." People often want to talk about activism, but sometimes I wonder if it's a test to see if an activist like me *really* loves Jesus and is theologically orthodox, or if I've been co-opted by some liberal influences. And believe me, being a graduate student at the University of Chicago doesn't relieve their worries.

Growing up in an evangelical church, I'd heard people say things like, "I'm about social Jesus, not social justice" and that conversations about racial justice seem to be misplacing one's identity in their race when it should be in Christ. I started getting involved with activism as a self-searching endeavor, defying the white evangelical culture I had grown up in. Having come from a troubled background, my church felt like a new beginning. I had found new friends, new ways of speaking, and new ways of thinking in my evangelical church. But in the process I realized that I had distanced myself so much from where I had come from. My testimony became a devotion, a creed if you will, that I would tell myself and others to remind them of how bad things were *there* (in the neighborhood I grew up in) and how good things are *here* (in this suburban hub called church). My transition into white evangelical culture was interpreted as a *road to Damascus* story, where everything associated with my former life was *bad* until I was hit by the evangelical Jesus who changed my life on the road to perdition.

When I spent time around childhood friends and family, I treated friends like "ministries" to me because my church told me they were. I told myself I had something special to "impart" and "share" with them that I didn't have before I started coming to their church. I couldn't figure out what that "what" was, but I called it "Jesus," despite the fact that most of my neighbors and friends were already self-identifying believers. I then considered my distinctive gift offering to be education, despite the fact that I wasn't a specialized educator whatsoever. Finally, I considered my distinctive gift to be morality, despite the fact that my basic moral impulses were shaped and influenced by people from within this community. I reached the height of my pride as an evangelical. I believed what was fundamentally in need of redemption in my old neighborhood was "moral culture." Now I realize that the only gift I imparted was condescension and false aspirations. I didn't realize that the testimony I told myself was a testimony of prosperity that implicitly said, "Access to people like this indicates your spiritual strength."

In other words, I told myself that in order to be a Christian, I had to express a shallow concern about the conditions my friends and family were living in and market my testimony as their salvation. But eventually, my heart caught up to me as well as my shame.

I would often approach coffee with white evangelicals confident that they'd see themselves as either saviors or grievers too. As saviors, they would market stories (like my own) to show how Jesus was working in and through *their* church through *their* leadership. I can't tell you how often my brown face became a prop among a sea of white faces to illustrate racial charity. As grievers, evangelicals would say, "I'm grieved by that, but we are called to pray. We are not called to be political."

And that is what made approaching the coffee conversation worrisome. It is difficult to push evangelicals to adopt bolder stances toward justice, which are tougher to achieve and keep them from self-congratulation. Now when I approach coffee, I keep it simple: just be honest. Tell them a story about a time you protested and what it meant to you. I typically begin with the time I heard of Laquan McDonald.

LAQUAN MCDONALD

On October 20, 2014, the Chicago police responded to a call involving a seventeen year old, Laquan McDonald, who was said to be behaving erratically while walking down the street and carrying a knife. The situation came to a sudden stop when Laquan was shot and killed by Officer Jason Van Dyke. Van Dyke alleged McDonald lunged at him with his knife and that the use of force was necessary.

Thirteen months after the event, dashcam footage was released to the public after a widespread dispute about the initial police report and the actual events. The video shown to the public was shocking. McDonald hadn't lunged at Officer Van Dyke. Instead, he was walking away from Van Dyke who emptied his sixteen-round magazine into Laquan's body just moments after he got out of his squad car. Although the video had been seen by Rahm Emmanuel (the mayor), Anita Alvarez (the State's Attorney), and Garry McCarthy (the superintendent of CPD), they all had deliberately suppressed the video for thirteen months.

The footage sparked protests around the city. One such protest took place on Black Friday in Chicago's busiest shopping district: Michigan Avenue. The idea behind the protest was to disrupt business as usual. A child was murdered by the police, and the city lied about it. We cannot continue with business as usual or escape the truth by shopping.

My wife and I decided to go. It was cold, but we were determined to make a difference. As we marched down Michigan Avenue, the cold faces of shoppers and police officers were fixed onto us. We knew what they were thinking: *Why are they making such a big deal? What change are they even enacting? Why are they choosing to disrupt ordinary people who just want to do their holiday shopping?*

About an hour into the demonstration, the organizers suggested that we line up in front of store entrances and lock arms. We made room behind us for shoppers who were determined to go inside, but we didn't want to give the slightest impression that our peaceful protest would be passive.

My wife and I locked arms in front of Victoria's Secret, a then profiteer of inmate labor. Angry shoppers confronted us with mean stares and insults. Others yelled at us, expressing their disdain by shouting, "You aren't helping your cause!" and "All Lives Matter!"

But one particular moment of the protest was sobering. There was a black security guard working at the Victoria's Secret. He was tall and slim, groomed well, and spoke respectfully to us protestors blocking the entranceway to his store. He guided shoppers behind us to the space we left for those eager to do their purchasing. At one moment one of the younger protestors turned to him and said, "You should be standing out here with us! They could shoot any one of us next, including you!"

His head sunk in shame and he began explaining to us how he had a daughter to take care of. I cringed as I realized he felt the need to explain why he needed to work and how he's just trying to get by. He was shamed by a "woke" protestor who, presumably, had the time to take off of work and the energy to protest.

Shortly after, others yelled at the woke shamer in response, "He's got children to feed! What is wrong with you shaming him?" Here he was: doing his job, trying to feed his family, while some college kid shamed him for it. I felt for the family man at Victoria's Secret.

For some, activism is an act of desperation—a last resort. For some, like our shaming friend, it is a function of privilege. For the Christian, however, it is an expression of *witness*. As an expression of witness, it takes seriously the fact that we are sinful creatures in a fallen world that are restored by God alone. Even as we stood against police brutality, government corruption, and other forms of injustice, our friend at Victoria's Secret could not stand with us. He himself is a reminder that the good we do is incomplete and that we are more steeped in sin and pretense than we originally thought. In other words, Christian witness carries within it a tragic sensibility.

This tragic sense lives with us by way of our historical parents: Adam and Eve. We inherit a past that weighs down on us in the present. This history is what Christians refer to as sin. We inherit this history from birth and cannot escape it no matter how much we fight against it.

Sin, therefore, is not merely the result of outside forces, capricious gods, or unjust politicians and police officers. For Christians, the tragic is not merely something that we *do* or something that *happens* to us; it is something we *are*. When we look inside ourselves, we find that we are broken vessels who are just in need of God's grace as anyone else. Christian activism is a tragic act of loving a broken world with our broken hearts. If this is the case, then our activism will always fall short of its goal to heal a broken world.

Silencing our tragic sense or remaining unaware of it causes us to rely more heavily on ourselves and to become self-righteous martyrs. In other words, pride is the greatest temptation of all activists. Pride will often compel us to believe history lies in our hands. It tells us that as long as the family men who sell out by working at Victoria's Secret do not join us in our struggle, then justice will never be attained. Pride can make one believe that the work we do is the most pristine. It gives us a false sense of security. But the Christian gospel says we cannot save ourselves. I am a liar and a deceiver; just like the men and women who suppressed that video. We are broken people living in a broken world trying to love broken people with our broken hearts. We all know how this works out; it's hard. We experience joy and pain, compassion and heartache, gain and loss. To experience deliverance from this history of bondage is to receive God's grace and trust that history's redemption is in the Lord's hands, not ours.

But one will rightfully ask, Does our tragic sensibility paralyze us from engagement with the world? I mean, if we are sinful, then why try? When activism runs up against its historical limitations, we don't need to fall into the trap of retreatism. Yes, *God* is the one with the last and final word, but God's Spirit empowers us to speak God's word to the world. God gives us the grace we need when we least expect it to continue on.

One afternoon, a student stopped by my office at a Christian institution I had been working at to ask me if I would be interested in speaking on a panel about the role of white allies for racial justice. I had just been at the protest and wasn't in the mood for teaching white people how to not be racist.

"I'm not really interested in this conversation," I said. "It places white guilt and discomfort at the center, where black and brown folks have to cater once again and police their tone. I hate when people police my tone. Black passion and rage are central to any discussion about injustice because it enlivens the black interlocutor with humanity; it legitimizes their emotion as a natural part of who they are and what they've endured. Any suppression of that in the name of civility is racist. And to be honest—I think I'm done with panels. I've sat on quite a few already these past eight months. I'm not interested in convincing anyone that white supremacy is a thing or why Black Lives Matter. That's someone else's conversation for someone else's patience. God bless 'em. I think I'm going to keep my conversations on racial justice and activism with people who actually care: folks from my neighborhood, my church, or something. Gotta encourage the saints, as we used to say in church. Discipleship, you know?"

"Can I tell you something?"

"Sure."

"I was at that protest in Chicago you went to."

"For real?"

"Yeah, I had never done anything like that before. I never would have thought I'd find anything like that in a Christian community, especially here. It took me by surprise. It's something I'll take with me forever."

"Wow. Thanks for sharing that with me."

"Yeah, when you rallied Christians online to come, I felt I needed to be there. We need to be challenged. We need to be disturbed. We need to know that there are different ways of being Christian that are meaningful to different people. That's what that protest was for me. And I really think you could challenge and encourage us if you came. You can say exactly what you just said to me now. But no pressure, though."

I pulled out my calendar—"Yeah, I'll be there."

Often when we think that the work we are doing is in vain, the Lord gives us another portion to continue going, to not grow weary in doing good, and that in due time we reap the harvest if we do not give up.

Not long after I shared on the panel had I received news that the district state's attorney had lost her bid for reelection and that Superintendent Garry McCarthy was fired. The *Chicago Tribune* noted that protests cost the city of Chicago 25-50 percent of sales. Shortly after that, we found out that Mayor Rahm Emmanuel would not seek reelection and that Jason Van Dyke was found guilty for second-degree murder. Princeton professor Keeanga-Yamahtta Taylor wrote that "justice is not a natural part of the lifecycle of the United States, nor is it a product of evolution; it is the outcome of struggle."[1] Had Christians decided to withdraw from activism under the pretext that "justice belongs to God," they would have misunderstood activism as *witness*. Christian activism is neither naive humanism nor passive retreatism; it is neither self-righteousness nor apathy. Christian activism is about *witness*—nothing more, nothing less.

MICAH 6:8

But what does witness *look like*? I think the prophet Micah addresses this question well in one of his most famous excerpts:

> He has shown you, O mortal, what is good.
>   And what does the LORD require of you?
> To act justly and to love mercy
>   and to walk humbly with your God.

To act justly. Christian witness means living out the life of the just reign of God. What does it mean to act justly? Justice is about fairness, orderliness, and compassion toward the most vulnerable within society—the Laquan McDonalds of the world. The Bible is a story about God's love and compassion for nothings, nobodies, and those without being. God creates the world out of love and for no other reason. God was neither lonely nor insecure, and God willed to create a world and people he can be in relationship with. God's creation rebelled against him, and the world spiraled out of control. A man becomes enraged with envy and kills his brother. The world caves in on itself, violence runs rampant, sinfulness pervades the creation, and the culmination of sinfulness climaxes in humanity's pride (Gen 11). Out of the depths of God's wisdom and love, God embarks on a mission to rescue his creation, to restore order and fairness—in a word, justice!—to his creation. He makes a covenant with a man named Abraham (Gen 12) and promises to redeem the once-purely-good, now-awry world. Through Abraham's descendants, God decides to form a people through whom the world will be blessed and reconciled by to their Creator.

The people God chose, however, also rebel against him. They ask for a king, neglecting the sovereign reign that God provided for them (1 Sam 8). Even through their rejection of God as King, God makes another covenant with his people—promising to bring about a Messiah who will usher in the eternal kingdom of God (2 Sam 7).

They commit acts of wickedness and they pervert justice; they worship other gods and they continuously mock their Creator. God punishes them for their disobedience, but he never breaks his promise to restore the world gone awry and usher in the kingdom where there is no more murder, no more coverups, no more perversion of justice, and the abolishment of distinctions intended to elevate ourselves and subjugate others.

God even extends the invitation to Abraham's seed by calling us "children of Abraham" (Gal 3:7, 29). God's mission is to restore justice to a world where men and women sworn to protect and serve regularly murder unarmed black men and women with impunity. Even more exciting, God calls us citizens of this kingdom and members of the family that God is forming together. God calls us to eat at his table and to remember his faithful love toward us.

One of the ways that we remember his faithful love toward us is by joining God's mission to the world. The people of God are faithful lovers of justice to the world, just as God is. We pray, sing songs of worship, and share our faith (which is an invitation to join the family), but the defining marker of our faith is our compassion and justice for the world, which witnesses to God's kingdom.

Jesus said (quoting Is 61:1-2):

The Spirit of the Lord is upon Me,

Because He has anointed Me

To preach the gospel to *the* poor.

He has sent Me to proclaim release to the captives,

And recovery of sight to the blind,

To set free those who are oppressed,

To proclaim the favorable year of the LORD. (Lk 4:18-19 NASB)

We are God's people—made to look like Jesus in every way. We are his new covenant people, empowered by the Spirit to "preach the gospel to the poor," "proclaim release to the captives," "recovery of sight to the blind," "to set free those who are oppressed," and "proclaim the favorable year of the Lord." We are created by this faithful lover who didn't give up on the world he created. But, rather, he pursued it in love and sought justice and peace for it relentlessly. We should too.

Part of the work of doing justice involves *exposing* and *attacking lies.* What would have happened if Laquan's death remained hidden from the public eye? Many would have maintained their assumption that activists are just "looking for something to be upset about" or that they are "overblowing a situation" and "creating division" by "demonizing" police. *Exposing lies* in this instance not only exposed the lie that Laquan hadn't lunged at Officer Van Dyke; it attacked the lie that police always tell the truth. One of the reasons that exposing police violence is unsettling for so many is because American police have been divinized in mainstream discourse.

Michelle Alexander, the author of *The New Jim Crow*, mentions heroic police dramas, such as *Law & Order*, which portray

a charismatic police officer, investigator or prosecutor [who] struggles with his own demons while heroically trying to solve a horrible crime.

He ultimately achieves a personal and moral victory by finding the bad guy and throwing him in jail. That is the made-for-TV version of the criminal justice system. It perpetuates the myth that the primary function of the system is to keep our streets safe and our homes secure by rooting out dangerous criminals and punishing them.[2]

When we expose the lie of police divinization and criminal demonization, we restore agency to both parties. One of the surest ways to divide humanity down an even line of good and bad guys is to strip them all of their own agency. However, the Christian message is that human beings remain in a paradoxical situation of sinner-saint and that all of us need the grace and mercy of God.

Love mercy. Even in the midst of their rebellion, God continues to show his faithfulness to the world by making yet another covenant with his people. Because of their undying propensity for defiance, God promises to write his law on their hearts and to fill them with his Holy Spirit, thereby aiding them in their obedience to God to be a light to the nations. God loves the world and is relentlessly pursuing the restoration of the world in love. The Creator chose to step into his creation and inaugurate a new one, where sin is obliterated and the presence of justice pervades the world. His Holy Spirit was poured out, and we begin to see glimpses of the world that is coming to consummate us in full. God, as Messiah, showed us miraculous healings, thereby showing us the imminent end to illness. God, as Messiah, spent the majority of his time among the poor and social pariahs, thereby showing us the imminent end to prejudice, injustice, and mercilessness in the kingdom.

We live in a punitive world. It is now well-known that the United States has the highest rate of incarceration in the world. We jail one-fourth of the world's prisoners, dish out mandatory minimum sentences to nonviolent offenders, and sentence children to die in prison. The politics of fear and anger, the desire to get tough on crime, and our desire for punitive justice says something about who we are as Americans. We are not merciful people. We are conditioned to be merciless, and that plays out in our personal lives. I want *every* offense against me to be punished. But mercy is restorative. When we punish others, we are effectively saying that this person is beyond restoration, that they cannot be restored in a humane way. When we punish others, we reduce others to their offense. We are essentially saying that they are *just* liars; they are *just* gossipers; they are *just* prideful.

In his book *Just Mercy*, Brian Stevenson, a renowned attorney who started the Equal Justice Initiative, makes a profound statement about the dignity of people and their need for mercy:

> Proximity has taught me some basic and humbling truths, including this vital lesson: Each of us is more than the worst thing we've ever done. My work with the poor and the incarcerated has persuaded me that the opposite of poverty is not wealth; the opposite of poverty is justice. Finally, I've come to believe that the true measure of our commitment to justice, the character of our society, our commitment to the rule of law, fairness, and equality cannot be measured by how we treat the rich, the powerful, the privileged, and the respected among us. The true measure of our character is how we treat the poor, the disfavored, the accused, the incarcerated, and the condemned.
>
> We are implicated when we allow other people to be mistreated. An absence of compassion can corrupt the decency of a community, a state, a nation. Fear and anger can make us vindictive and abusive, unjust and unfair, until we all suffer from the absence of mercy and we condemn ourselves as much as we victimize others. The closer we get to mass incarceration and extreme levels of punishment, the more I believe it's necessary to recognize that we all need mercy, we all need justice, and—perhaps—we all need some measure of unmerited grace.[3]

Sadly, Laquan McDonald was not afforded that same mercy and grace. And he is not an isolated incident. With the rise of social media, fatal encounters between black people and police have revealed how commonplace events like this are. And they manifest and entrench a deeper, *spiritual* malady—that our hearts can become hardened with *mercilessness*. The mercilessness of so many Americans rises to the surface when they ask in bad faith, "Why didn't they just cooperate with the officer?" or "What did they do *before* the camera was turned on to provoke them?" Everyone wants to believe that mercilessness is justified until it comes our way.

Scripture tells us to love mercy because we all need it. When we look at America's racial lockup craze, it is evident that mercy is only reserved for some. On January 18, 2019, Judge Vincent Gaughan sentenced Jason Van Dyke to eighty-one months in prison for second-degree murder and aggravated assault. His fellow officers who were initially responsible for covering up the murder were acquitted in their involvement. Judge Gaughan declared that the grief on both sides (for McDonald's family and Van Dyke's) was equally tragic.

After the sentencing, Tiffany Van Dyke, Jason's wife, said, "I am thankful the judge showed some mercy for Jason." But is it fair to characterize *bias* as mercy? Mercy should be indiscriminate, cutting across racial, class, ethnic, and religious lines. The mercy God pours out that we are called to witness to is a universal one. The mercy and grace the Scriptures point to are given *especially* to those most often denied it on this side of heaven.

Walk humbly with God. The McDonald case is tragic because it shows the relative progress made through activism. No doubt, organizations like BYP100 (Black Youth Project 100), Assata's Daughters, and Black Lives Matter have been crucial in the active effort to secure the safety and justice of Chicago's most vulnerable. But much of their efforts runs up against recalcitrance. And that has been the case for centuries. The civil rights era may have brought school segregation and police brutality to the public's eye, but racism and police brutality are as alive today as they were then.

And the more we consider this tragic aspect of Christian activism in an unjust world, the more we come to realize that we need the Spirit of God to revive, encourage, and embolden our witness. Otherwise, why try? We cannot change the world, but that is not cause for despair. We have a God who promises to never leave nor forsake us as we witness to his eternal reign of justice. The tragedy is that we are not promised to see the fruit of our labor, but the hope is that God has the last and final word. To walk humbly with God is to recognize our weakness in relation to God's strength. It is not to accept defeat, for that would entail walking *from* God. Walking *with* God is sharing in God's commitment to the world while acknowledging that God is its sole Redeemer.

CONCLUSION

The coffee conversation can go in different directions after all this. For some, all they've heard is "police are bad" and they check out after that. Others, however, are moved in their soul. And I'm surprised by how often people of all ages ask me the same question: Why aren't Christians doing something about these injustices? It's a good question, filled with genuine concern about the spiritual vitality of the church and its mission. But perhaps a better way of asking the question is: *Who* are the Christians doing something about these injustices?

When we ask this question, we discover a world of courageous Christians who stood up, spoke out, and trusted that God walked with them in their faithful witness to his reign. We come to find that God does not leave the world without prophets and that sometimes we are blessed in our lifetimes to be disturbed by them. We are reminded of the faithful witnesses of Dietrich Bonhoeffer, Óscar Romero, and Fannie Lou Hamer. But we also find that we currently live in a world of courageous Christians like Cornel West, Renita Green, and Larycia Hawkins—people who show us now how to live justly, love mercy, and walk humbly with God today. May our cup also overflow with justice, mercy, and humility to be poured out in the world that God loves. In those times that coffee goes well, we both ask for a refill.

Notes

PREFACE

[1]Gary M. Burge and David Lauber, *Theology Questions Everyone Asks: Christian Faith in Plain Language* (Downers Grove, IL: InterVarsity Press, 2014).

1 COMMUNITY AND FRIENDSHIP

[1]In truth, Beth is a composite of the stories of about eight students I know well. Each feature of her story is a feature of one of these students. And yet her profile generally will be immediately recognizable to most college students today.

[2]Dietrich Bonhoeffer, *Life Together*, trans. J. W. Doberstein (New York: Harper & Row, 1954), 19.

[3]Bonhoeffer, *Life Together*, 23.

[4]Christine D. Pohl, *Living into Community: Cultivating Practices That Sustain Us* (Grand Rapids: Eerdmans, 2011).

[5]Christine D. Pohl, *Making Room: Recovering Hospitality as a Christian Tradition* (Grand Rapids: Eerdmans, 1999).

[6]Pohl, *Living into Community*, 150.

2 VOCATION

[1]William C. Placher, ed., *Callings: Twenty Centuries of Christian Wisdom on Vocation* (Grand Rapids: Eerdmans, 2005).

[2]For more on this topic, see Austin Channing Brown, *I'm Still Here: Black Dignity in a World Made for Whiteness* (New York: Convergent, 2018); Adrian Pei, *The Minority Experience* (Downers Grove, IL: InterVarsity Press, 2018); and Jemar Tisby, *The Color of Compromise: The Truth About the American Church's Complicity in Racism* (Grand Rapids: Zondervan, 2019).

[3]For more on choice paralysis and anticipated regret, see chapter seven of Barry Schwartz, *Paradox of Choice: Why More Is Less* (New York: HarperCollins, 2016).

[4]There are many excellent books available to learn more about practicing the traditional spiritual disciplines. Dallas Willard's *The Spirit of the Disciplines* (New York: HarperCollins, 1999) and Tish Harrison Warren, *Liturgy of the Ordinary: Sacred Practices in Everyday Life* (Downers Grove, IL: InterVarsity Press, 2016) would be great places to start. Rebecca DeYoung's *Glittering Vices* (Grand Rapids: Brazos, 2009), a book on the closely related topic of virtues, is also very good. I also particularly like Kyle David Bennett's *Practices of Love: Spiritual Disciplines for the Life of the World* (Grand Rapids: Brazos, 2017).

[5]Bennett, *Practices of Love*, 9.

[6]Bennett, *Practices of Love*, 9.

[7]C. S. Lewis, *The Weight of Glory and Other Addresses* (Grand Rapids: Eerdmans, 1949), 15.

3 GENDER ROLES

[1]Frederick C. Bauerschmidt, "The Trinity," in *Gathered for the Journey: Moral Theology in Catholic Perspective*, ed. David Matzko McCarthy and M. Therese Lysaught (Grand Rapids: Eerdmans, 2007), 85.

[2]John Walton, *Genesis*, NIV Application Commentary (Grand Rapids: Zondervan, 2001), 176.

[3]See, for example, the text edited by John Piper and Wayne Grudem, *Recovering Biblical Manhood and Womanhood: A Response to Evangelical Feminism* (Wheaton, IL: Crossway, 2012).

[4]For further reading, see Scot McKnight, *The Blue Parakeet: Rethinking How You Read the Bible*, 2nd ed. (Grand Rapids: Zondervan, 2018).

[5]Katelyn Beaty, *A Woman's Place: A Christian Vision for Your Calling in the Office, the Home, and the World* (New York: Howard Books, 2016), 99.

[6]Stephanie Coontz, *The Way We Never Were: American Families and the Nostalgia Trap* (New York: Basic Books, 2000), 53.

[7]Jennifer Szalai, "The Complicated Origins of 'Having It All,'" *New York Times Magazine*, January 2, 2015, www.nytimes.com/2015/01/04/magazine/the-complicated-origins-of-having-it-all.html.

[8]Arlie Hochschild and Anne Machung, *The Second Shift: Working Families and the Revolution at Home*, 3rd ed. (New York: Penguin Books, 2012).

[9]Beaty, *Woman's Place*, 157.

[10]Nikki Graf, Anna Brown, and Eileen Patten, "The Narrowing, but Persistent, Gender Gap in Pay," Pew Research Center, April 9, 2018, www.pewresearch.org/fact-tank/2018/04/09/gender-pay-gap-facts.

[11]Beaty, *Woman's Place*, 65-66.

[12]Frederick Buechner, *Wishful Thinking: A Seeker's ABC* (San Francisco: HarperOne, 1993), 118.

5 MARRIAGE

[1]Lawrence B. Finer, "Trends in Premarital Sex in the United States, 1954-2003," *Public Health Reports* 122 (January-February 2007).

[2]See, for example, John Eldredge, *Wild at Heart: Discovering the Secret of a Man's Soul* (Nashville: Thomas Nelson, 2006); John Eldredge and Staci Eldredge, *Captivating: Unveiling the Mystery of a Woman's Soul* (Nashville: Thomas Nelson, 2005); Joshua Harris, *I Kissed Dating Goodbye: A New Attitude Toward Romance and Relationships* (Colorado Springs, CO: Multnomah, 2003); Eric Ludy and Leslie Ludy, *When God Writes Your Love Story: The Ultimate Approach to Guy/Girl Relationships*, exp. ed. (Colorado Springs, CO: Multnomah, 2009); Leslie Ludy, *Authentic Beauty: The Shaping of a Set-Apart Young Woman* (Colorado Springs, CO: Multnomah, 2007); and Heather Arnel Paulsen, *Emotional Purity: An Affair of the Heart* (Wheaton, IL: Crossway, 2007).

[3]Much of the material from this and the preceding paragraph first appeared in Margaret Kim Peterson and Dwight M. Peterson, *Are You Waiting for "the One"? Cultivating Realistic, Positive Expectations for Christian Marriage* (Downers Grove, IL: InterVarsity Press, 2011), 31-32.

6 CHURCH

[1]Cyprian, *On the Unity of the Church* 6, in *Ante-Nicene Fathers*, ed. Philip Schaff (Peabody, MA: Hendrickson, 1995), 5:423.

[2]John Calvin, *The Institutes of the Christian Religion* 4.1.4, ed. John T. McNeill, trans. Ford Lewis Battles (Philadelphia: Westminster Press, 1960), 1016.

7 WEALTH AND POWER

[1]Basil the Great, quoted in Nicholas Wolterstorff, *Journey toward Justice: Personal Encounters in the Global South* (Grand Rapids: Baker, 2013), 66.

[2]Emmanuel Katongole and Chris Rice, *Reconciling All Things: A Christian Vision for Justice, Peace, and Healing* (Downers Grove, IL: IVP Academic, 2008), 87.

[3]Katongole and Rice, *Reconciling All Things*, 85.

[4]Karen A. Longman, *Diversity Matters: Race, Ethnicity, and the Future of Christian Higher Education* (Abilene, TX: Abilene Christian University Press, 2017).

[5]Samuel Bowles, Eric Alden Smith, and Monique Borgerhoff Molder, "The Emergence and Persistence of Inequality in Premodern Societies," *Current Anthropology* 51, no.1 (2010): 9.

[6]Luke Eric Lassiter, *Invitation to Anthropology* (Lanham, MD: Rowman & Littlefield, 2014), 216.

[7]Andy Crouch, *Playing God: Redeeming the Gift of Power* (Downers Grove, IL: InterVarsity Press, 2013).

[8]Richard J. Foster, *The Challenge of the Disciplined Life: Christian Reflections on Money, Sex, & Power* (New York: HarperCollins, 1985), 24.

[9]Foster, *Challenge of the Disciplined Life*, 24-25.

[10]Chimamanda Ngozi Adichie, "The Danger of the Single Story," *TED.com*, July 2009, www.ted.com/talks/chimamanda_adichie_the_danger_of_a_single_story.

[11]Matthew Desmond, *Evicted: Poverty and Profit in the American City* (New York: Penguin, 2016), 317.

[12]Vincent Miller, *Consuming Religion: Christian Faith and Practice in a Consumer Culture*, quoted in Ruth Valero, *Just Living: Faith and Community in an Age of Consumerism* (London: Hodder & Stoughton, 2016), 63.

[13]Valero, *Just Living*, 242.

[14]Bryan Stevenson, *Just Mercy* (New York: Penguin, 2015).

[15]Foster, *Challenge of the Disciplined Life*, 28.

[16]Foster, *Challenge of the Disciplined Life*, 176.

[17]Foster, *Challenge of the Disciplined Life*, 39.

[18]Foster, *Challenge of the Disciplined Life*, 196.

[19]Foster, *Challenge of the Disciplined Life*, 71.

[20]Foster, *Challenge of the Disciplined Life*, 72.

[21]Foster, *Challenge of the Disciplined Life*, 73.

[22]Foster, *Challenge of the Disciplined Life*, 228.

[23]Foster, *Challenge of the Disciplined Life*, 230.

[24]Foster, *Challenge of the Disciplined Life*, 229.

[25]Henri J. M. Nouwen, Donald P. McNeil, and Douglas A. Morrison, *Compassion: A Reflection on the Christian Life* (New York: Doubleday, 1982), 4.

[26]Foster, *Challenge of the Disciplined Life*, 87.

[27]Dallas Willard, *The Divine Conspiracy: Rediscovering Our Hidden Life in God* (New York: HarperCollins, 1998), 208.

8 SUFFERING

[1]C. S. Lewis, *A Grief Observed* (San Francisco: HarperOne, 1961), 22.

[2]J. Todd Billings, *Rejoicing in Lament: Wrestling with Incurable Cancer and Life in Christ* (Grand Rapids: Brazos Press, 2015), 86-89.

[3]Billings, *Rejoicing in Lament*, 87. Wright's quote comes from his *Evil and the Justice of God* (Downers Grove, IL: InterVarsity, 2006), 55.

[4]In his Heidelberg Disputation, the sixteenth-century Reformer Martin Luther draws a distinction between a theology of glory and a theology of the cross. A theology of the cross "comprehends the visible and manifest things of God seen through suffering and the cross," while a theology of glory "prefers works to suffering, glory to the cross, strength to weakness." According to Luther, the true theologian must be a theologian of the cross. A theology of the cross stresses God's power as seen in the

apparent weakness of Christ crucified, while a theology of glory focuses on one's own strength and self-sufficient power. Martin Luther, *Martin Luther's Basic Theological Writings*, edited by Timothy F. Lull and William R. Russell, 3rd ed. (Minneapolis: Fortress Press, 2012), 14-25.

[5]Otis Moss III and Otis Moss Jr, "Prophetic Grief," *YouTube*, June 24, 2015, www .youtube.com/watch?v=EqImk7g2RD0.

9 DOUBT

[1]All Scripture quotations in this chapter are from the NRSV.

[2]Alvin Plantings, "Reason and Belief in God," in *Faith and Rationality: Reason and Belief in God*, ed. Alvin Plantings and Nicholas Wolterstorff (Notre Dame, IN: University of Notre Dame Press, 1984), 87.

[3]See Lesslie Newbigin, *Proper Confidence: Faith, Doubt, and Certainty in Christian Discipleship* (Grand Rapids: Eerdmans, 1995), 23-24.

[4]See Randall C. Zachman, *The Assurance of Faith: Conscience in the Theology of Martin Luther and John Calvin* (Minneapolis: Fortress Press, 1993), 63-68.

[5]John Calvin, commentary on Romans 4:20, in *Calvin's Commentaries: The Epistles of Paul the Apostle to the Romans and to the Thessalonians*, trans. Ross McKenzie, ed. David W. Torrance and Thomas F. Torrance (Grand Rapids: Eerdmans, 1994), 99.

[6]On this point, see Karl Barth, *Church Dogmatics* II/1 (Edinburgh: T&T Clark, 1957), 3-31.

[7]Charles Taylor, *A Secular Age* (Cambridge, MA: Belknap Press, 2007), 22.

[8]Timothy Keller, *The Reason for God: Belief in an Age of Skepticism* (New York: Dutton, 2008), xxxiii.

[9]Dietrich Bonhoeffer, *Discipleship*, trans. Martin Kuske and Isle Tödt, Dietrich Bonhoeffer Works 4 (Minneapolis: Fortress Press, 2001), 63-64.

10 COUNSELING

[1]Sumie Okazaki, "Impact of Racism on Ethnic Minority Mental Health," *Perspectives on Psychological Science* 4, no. 1 (2009), 103-7, https://doi.org/10.1111/j.1745-6924 .2009.01099.x.

[2]Stanton Jones and Richard Butman, *Modern Psychotherapies: A Comprehensive Christian Appraisal* (Downers Grove, IL: IVP Academic, 2011).

[3]Mark McMinn and Clark Campbell, *Integrative Psychotherapy: Toward a Comprehensive Christian Approach* (Downers Grove, IL: InterVarsity Press, 2007); Mark Yarhouse and James Sells, *Family Therapies: A Comprehensive Christian Appraisal*, 2nd ed. (Downers Grove, IL: IVP Academic, 2017); and Stanton Jones and Richard Butman, *Modern Psychotherapies: A Comprehensive Christian Appraisal* (Downers Grove, IL: IVP Academic, 2011).

[4]Christian hope is distinctive because through grace we can experience hope as a theological virtue, meaning that our character can be ennobled in a way that surpasses what we could be of ourselves (Josef Pieper, *Faith, Hope, Love* [San Francisco: Ignatius Press, 1997], 99). As a psychologist interested in thinking patterns, I like the idea that virtues are also habits. They're something we can practice, with virtue slowly becoming our default response. Hence, hope is something supplied by grace and we can participate with God's work by practicing hope. A number of theologians use the term *status viatoris* or the state of a person being "on the way" to describe Christians. This means our path is oriented toward our ultimate fulfillment in heaven (91-95). The things we hope for on the way can serve to remind us of our ultimate hope in Christ.

11 RELIGIOUS PLURALISM

[1]Christian Smith and Melinda Lundquist Denton, *Soul Searching: The Religious and Spiritual Lives of American Teenagers* (Oxford: Oxford University Press, 2005), 162-71.

[2]Francis of Assisi, "St. Francis of Assisi Prayer: Showing the World a Way Out," *PrayRay*, accessed March 17, 2020, https://prayray.com/st-francis-of-assisi-prayer.

[3]Augustine, *Confessions* 1.1.1, trans. Henry Chadwick (Oxford: Oxford University Press, 2009), 3.

[4]Peter Kreeft, quoted in Justin Taylor, "An Analysis of One of the Greatest Sentences Ever Written," *Gospel Coalition* (blog), accessed March 9, 2017, www.thegospelco alition.org/blogs/justin-taylor/an-analysis-of-one-of-the-greatest-sentences-ever -written.

[5]David Kinnaman and Gabe Lyons, *unChristian: What a New Generation Really Thinks about Christianity . . . and Why It Matters* (Grand Rapids: Baker, 2007), 186-95.

[6]David B. Capes, *Slow to Judge: Sometimes It's OK to Listen* (Nashville: Thomas Nelson, 2015), xxix.

[7]See the excellent biography of Lewis: Alistair McGrath, *C. S. Lewis—A Life: Eccentric Genius, Reluctant Prophet* (Carol Stream, IL: Tyndale, 2013).

[8]C. S. Lewis, *Mere Christianity* (New York: HarperOne, 2000), 35. When Lewis wrote, the term *queer* meant "odd" or "strange"; it had nothing to do with sexual orientation.

[9]Capes, *Slow to Judge*, 131-32.

[10]C. S. Lewis, "Myth Became Fact," in *God in the Dock: Essays on Theology and Ethics* (Grand Rapids: Eerdmans, 1971), 64.

[11]Michael Ward, "The Good Serves the Better and Both the Best: C. S. Lewis on Imagination and Reason in Apologetics," in *Imaginative Apologetics: Theology, Philosophy and the Catholic Tradition*, ed. Andrew Davison (Grand Rapids: Baker Academic, 2011), 65.

[12]Michael J. Gorman, *Becoming the Gospel: Paul, Participation, and Mission* (Grand Rapids: Eerdmans, 2015).

12 ACTIVISM

[1]Keeanga-Yamahtta Taylor, *From #BlackLivesMatter to Black Liberation* (Chicago, Illinois: Haymarket Books, 2016), 5.

[2]Michelle Alexander, *Mass Incarceration in the Age of Colorblindness* (New York: New Press, 2010), 59.

[3]Bryan Stevenson, *Just Mercy: A Story of Justice and Redemption* (New York: Spiegel & Grau, 2014), 17-18.

Scripture Index